Emotion in Social Life

Emphasis Social Life

Emotion in Social Life

The Lost Heart of Society

Derek Layder

⑤ SAGE Publications

London ● Thousand Oaks ● New Delhi

SAGE Publications Ltd
1 Oliver's Yard
55 City Road
London EC1Y 1SP

SAGE Publications Inc
2455 Teller Road
Thousand Oaks, California 91320

SAGE Publications India Pvt Ltd
B-42, Panchsheel Enclave
Post Box 4109
New Delhi 110 017

British Library Cataloguing in Publication data

A catalogue record for this book is available from the British Library

ISBN 0 7619 4365 X
ISBN 0 7619 4366 8

Library of Congress control number available

Typeset by C&M Digitals (P) Ltd., Chennai, India
Printed in Great Britain by Athenaeum Press, Gateshead

Contents

Introduction: Uncovering the Lost Heart   1

1   Theoretical Issues   7

2   The Psychology of Personal Control   24

3   Social Encounters   38

4   Types and Dimensions   59

5   Familiar Issues and Examples   66

6   Failures of Control   89

7   Some Propositions about Human Behaviour   104

8   The Lost Heart: Theory and Research   115

References   122

Index   125

Introduction

Uncovering the Lost Heart

This book is about interpersonal control in modern society and its close relation to our emotional lives – our feelings and responses. What is interpersonal control? The 'interpersonal' part of the phrase refers to the mutuality of our relationships with others. We don't and can't 'do' personal relationships on our own. To a large extent, how we respond or deal with a friend or lover, or even a stranger, will depend upon how we think they will respond to us. We take them into account by anticipating their behaviour towards us, while at the same time they are similarly engaged. The other part of the phrase directs attention to the fact that interpersonal relations involve mutual control.

Initially, many people respond to the idea that they are involved in attempting to control others by outright denial. This is because we commonly think of control as negative behaviour associated with harming others or making them do something against their wishes. However, 'control' and even 'manipulation' may be understood in softer, kinder and more compassionate terms. This involves getting others to do what you would like them to do *willingly*, through influence, persuasion and charm by convincing them that it is in their interests.

Getting someone to go out on a date, trying to impress others in a conversation, persuading your partner to spend more quality time with you, even convincing an elderly person to lock up securely at night are all examples in which 'benign' forms of control and manipulation play a part. Instead of deceiving or forcing others, we adopt a sympathetic and caring attitude rather than an exploitative one. Moreover, the person being controlled is free to resist and may only be finally 'won over' through further persuasion or inducement. This differs markedly from exploitative control, which is less easily questioned and in which resistance or reluctance to comply is typically overcome by threats or punishment.

While we recognize the existence of the more exploitative forms of control in modern life (and as far as is possible, try to keep them at arm's length), we tend to overlook the continuous influence of benign control in every facet of our daily lives. It is ever-present in ordinary conversations, in arguments or in the way we try to impress others, as well as in the myriad of ways in which we try to help each other out in daily life. It is just as common in the workplace and in careers as it is in our more personal 'private' lives. These are the kinds of setting which form the backdrop of situated activity in which different kinds and strategies of interpersonal control take place. In this sense it is the presence of other people and our interactions with them that fully reveal the true nature of our personal and social relationships.

This book examines the many ways in which power and control – both 'benign' and 'exploitative' – influence daily life, the quality of your relationships and your feelings. In this respect interpersonal control and the situated activities in which they are embedded represent the real heart of society. So much of the business of social life is conducted in terms of interpersonal relations (and situated activity) and as a consequence the elements of control implicit in them take on great importance. But I also argue that it is precisely this area that to a great extent has been, and continues to be, neglected in sociological analysis for reasons I shall spell out presently. This brings us back to the sub-title of this book. The 'lost heart' of society refers to the manner in which interpersonal control has been 'lost' to sociological analysis.

Why lost? There are four main reasons or sets of issues pertinent to this depiction. First, theoretical strands of sociological analysis have produced two very contrasting attitudes. One strand eliminates this area of social life as a domain in its own right altogether. The other strand corrals and isolates interpersonal control from other crucial social influences. In either case a proper understanding of the heart of society is hampered and hence 'lost'. Second, sociological analysis has concentrated on certain features of power (mainly its macro and/or discursive elements) to the exclusion of interpersonal power and control. Third, dominant trends in social research have understated the importance of interpersonal control and allowed it to slip through the net of typical research strategies. Finally, the links between emotion, power and interpersonal control have not been sufficiently emphasized and accorded the importance they deserve for grasping the inner heart of society.

The Incredible Shrinking Society

Interpersonal control is part of, and belongs to, the domain of situated activity – the encounters in which so much of the essential day-to-day business of social life is conducted. However, although it is a distinctive domain in its own right, situated activity does not stand alone as if it represented the whole of society or social reality. There are other domains associated with agency and subjective experience, as well as more objective ones referring to institutional, structural, systemic features of society. It is only in terms of the overall interlinking of these domains that what happens within and between each of them can be explained. None of them alone can account for the complexity and 'depth' of society (social reality) as a whole.

However, in Chapter 1 I argue that current attempts to resolve the agency–structure problem in social theory (which is basically about how agency and structure are interlinked) have resulted in the 'disappearance' of social domains and, hence, of large tracts of social reality (society). Typically, 'resolutions' of the agency–structure problem (and their conceptual frameworks) have focused around particular domains. But this very strategy requires that other aspects (domains) of social reality be ignored, overlooked or downgraded. In producing an artificially narrowed-down version of society, the study of interpersonal control (and, hence, its proper explanation) has been correspondingly impeded. Social theory has produced two distinct variations of this problem.

In the first the compaction and flattening of social reality have the effect of eliminating the existence of situated activity as a distinct and relatively autonomous domain. As a result, interpersonal control is ignored as an area of theoretical and empirical importance in its own right. The second version is almost the complete opposite of the first. Instead of ignoring situated activity, some theorists have exaggerated its importance out of all proportion by equating it with social reality as a whole. Thus a single domain comes to 'represent' all social phenomena.

The same flattening and compaction of social reality are involved, but the overall emphasis is reversed. Instead of eliminating it altogether, the domain has somehow been promoted to the only one of substantive and explanatory importance. Thus crucial subjective and objective domains are excluded from the picture. Both versions are unsatisfactory because they either cut out or overrate situated activity – the heart of much of the day-to-day business of society. Either way they contribute to the state of affairs alluded to in the phrase the 'lost heart' of society.

Interpersonal Control: Less than Middle-range Power?

A further reason why the core of interpersonal control at the heart of modern societies has been largely lost to sociological analysis is because sociologists have typically regarded power exclusively as a large-scale, structural phenomenon (even while maintaining that, in principle, power may also exist between individuals). Marx's treatment of class power and Weber's analysis of forms of power and authority remain steadfastly at the level of groups and institutions and have massively influenced subsequent sociological discussions about the nature of power. There are emphases in Simmel's work that point to the interpersonal level of analysis, but by comparison with the other two authors, Simmel's work – perhaps unfairly – has not had the same general impact and influence on sociological analysis.

Foucault is the modern author who stresses the centrality and importance of power. However, despite claiming that power reaches into the finest capillaries of society – to the level of the self and interpersonal relations – Foucault does not discuss or analyse everyday social interaction and hence is unable to properly account for power at this level. This is because he wrongly views power (and social reality in general) as exclusively discursive in form. Foucault's analysis shrinks society and social processes down to a concentration on discursive practices and the powers inscribed in them. As a consequence, the main problem is that he ignores or overlooks forms of power other than the discursive one of which he is so enamoured. But this is also because he overlooks other domains of social reality. In this sense Foucault's work is a prime example of the reductive strategies described in the previous section.

In sociology in general then (with the exception of interactionism), the analysis of interpersonal relations has often been obscured by a concentration on the more visible, large-scale, official institutional frontage of society. The fact is that interpersonal relations (and control) are somewhat less than middle-range in scale as compared with phenomena like class, gender, ethnicity, the state and bureaucracy that often take centrestage in social analysis. Thus even when interpersonal control does become a topic of analysis, it tends to be regarded as off-centre in relation to more important or 'central' foci of interest. But it is important to counter the assumption that processes associated with interpersonal control are somehow less crucial for the workings of society in general.

In fact the phenomena of interpersonal control play an integral role in the success or failure of more general cohesive and integrative processes in the social fabric. As such they underlie and provide infrastructural support for many of the more headline-grabbing social institutions and practices. They are the often obscured bedrock on which the larger and seemingly more important edifice of society rests. It is also important to recognize that interpersonal relations provide a point of connection and access to individual behaviour. Hence they can be understood as mediations and ligatures, tying subjective experience to the more objective elements of social settings, structures and systems.

Linking Theory and Social Research

The topic of interpersonal relations and control raises the question of the tendency for research on particular areas to be done discretely with a singular concentrated focus on the main topic. This overly directed stance has the effect of neglecting wider links between research and social theory. Two aspects of this are especially pertinent to the present discussion – the issues of comparative analysis and the connection between substantive and general theory.

Clearly, in terms of empirical research there have been studies that cover aspects of control in interpersonal relations. Research into women abuse either in the domestic environment or more generally is a good example, as is the analysis of communication within families. By concentrating on defined areas like these, such studies provide important and useful information about interpersonal processes. However, while a specific focus adds apparent depth to the research, it also diverts attention away from what may be important links between it and other areas.

Thus while there may be a growth in substantive knowledge and theory about such areas, there is no corresponding development of links with more general social theory which might serve to draw together knowledge over a wider terrain with the objective of building a coherent and far-ranging body of theoretical knowledge (Layder 1998). This book addresses the need to develop cumulative knowledge and general theory in this respect by analysing interpersonal phenomena over a range of areas that, although seemingly different, are related through the common link of control.

By so doing it is possible to develop models of the operation of interpersonal control by identifying different types and strategies of control and how they relate to one another. Theory so developed can be fed back into the research process by generating testable propositions about human social behaviour that are themed around the issue of control.

Emotion, Power and Control

Finally, the idea of interpersonal control as the lost heart of society is reflected in the relative neglect of the emotions in social analysis – although recently there has been an upsurge of interest in the topic. More than this, the deep-seated associations between power and the emotions have received some sporadic (and again, growing) acknowledgement. However, the same cannot be said with regard to recognizing the connection between emotion, control and interpersonal relations across a wide range of areas of social life.

It is necessary to acknowledge that the link between power and emotion is not simply contingent and haphazard. The two are to be found in each other's company in every instance. While, as Foucault observes, power can be said to be everywhere – in every nook and cranny of social existence – he fails to recognize that it manifests itself in quite different (and sometimes hybrid) forms in different social domains (for an extended argument, see Layder 1997). Similarly, being its constant companion, emotion is likewise ubiquitous, although often operating less obviously and visibly, underground.

There is a commonly held, but wrongly attributed, association between power and the negative emotions. This has something to do with the idea that power is inevitably about denial of freedom, of prohibition, limitation, even coercion and domination. Of course, these are at times characteristic of power and control, and as such, often elicit negative emotions such as anger, hatred, pain, shame and humiliation as well as the violence and abusiveness that inevitably accompany them.

A social domain view of the variable forms of power in conjunction with the comparative study of interpersonal control across a wide range of substantive areas makes it plain that the links between emotion and power and control are not simple, uniform or necessarily negative. Many areas of everyday life, including intimate relationships, are profoundly influenced by benign forms of (interpersonal) control that enable or facilitate one's own and others' purposes. In short, they expand or open up areas of freedom rather than close them down.

Along with this, the positive emotions – like care, pride, joy and fulfilment – become more visible and prominent. Although perhaps not a popular conclusion, it is nevertheless irresistible; fine emotions and feeling are the exquisite drapery of something apparently less fine and 'deserving', namely control, but this time in its mutual benign form. But again this area is destined to remain part of the lost heart of society as long as it goes unacknowledged in social analysis.

How the Book is Organized

This book may be read in slightly different ways according to the specific needs of the reader. A discussion of the practical and substantive issues associated with interpersonal control can be found in Chapters 4–7, which contain the main bulk of the discussion about types and strategies of control as well as illustrative examples. These chapters have a self-contained coherence and can, in principle, be read independently of the rest of the book. Those who are interested in the social and psychological theory relevant to interpersonal control will find this discussed in Chapters 2 and 3. Those who are interested in deeper issues of social analysis that furnish the wider context of the argument will also want to read Chapters 1 and 8. Chapter 1 unravels a bit more of the story concerning the agency–structure problem in social theory, while Chapter 8 returns to some wider questions about the links between theory and social research that flow from the more substantive issues that precede it.

Acknowledgements

Many People have contributed indirectly (although no less importantly) to my ability to write this book. In this regard, conversations with Mick Gardiner, Silvana DiGregorio and Mike Harper proved encouraging early on. More direct support came from Chris Rojek and Kay Bridger at Sage. The comments of three anonymous reviewers on the initial proposal were helpful and interesting. However, Doug Porpora's influence has been the most decisive. I'd like to thank him for his very perceptive and eminently constructive comments on an earlier version of the manuscript.

1

Theoretical Issues

Preview

- Social reality should be viewed in more encompassing terms – as multiple domains – in order to grasp the nature of interpersonal control.
- To understand social agency properly we need to recognize the variation in capacities and skills that emerge from individual psychobiographies.
- Agency, emotion and self-identity also have to be understood in the wider context of situated activity.
- The influence of social settings and wider contextual resources on interpersonal control.
- The importance of the dual nature of social relationships and multiple forms of power.
- Creativity and constraint in social life.
- The nature of social interaction and interpersonal control.

The term 'social relationship' refers to a fairly wide range of relationship types – from intimate, long-standing ties with friends, partners, spouses and other family members, to fleeting and relatively impersonal encounters with ticket clerks, car salespersons or local government workers. Regardless of how intimate they are, they all serve to remind us of our inescapably social nature. In order to understand our existence as unique individuals, we must abandon romantic ideas of ourselves as 'splendidly isolated' from others. While it is true that we are unique individuals, uniquely formed, the tentacles of modern society are so all-embracing that much of what we think – even our most private thoughts – and a great deal of what we do are strongly affected by the pervasive influence of our social environment.

Now these issues raise the question of the connection between the individual and society – what its exact nature is, and how we should account for it in an explanatory sense, and so on. This 'problem' has been at the centre of debate since sociology's inception as a discipline. More recently, what has become referred to as the 'agency–structure' problem has largely supplanted the more traditional question of the relationship between the individual and society.

It is probably true to say that the phrase 'agency–structure' is a more sophisticated expression of some of the theoretical issues involved. In particular it points to the creative capacities of human beings (agency or action), while also drawing attention to the fact that this creativity is worked out in the context of already established networks of social institutions and cultural and material resources. Thus the central topic of this book – interpersonal power and control – is importantly enmeshed in the more general theoretical and empirical problem of the relation between agency and structure.

Conceptual Singularities and their Black Holes

Much energy and debate has been invested in attempting to solve or resolve the agency–structure problem and I shall not rehearse these in any detail here (see Layder 1997, 2005 for critical assessments). However, at least some of the issues are of relevance to the topic of interpersonal control. Most important of these, perhaps, is the fact that many theorists who have dealt with this problem have replaced the dualism (of agency and structure) with some unitary conceptual meld of the elements involved.

The most common of these conceptual singularities involve reference to 'social practice or practices'. Giddens (1984), for example, speaks of 'reproduced social practices', Bourdieu (1977) of a 'theory of practice', Foucault (1980) of 'discursive practices', Garfinkel (1967) of 'local or artful practices'. But variations on the idea of practice are not mandatory. Elias's (1978) conceptual replacement for 'false dualisms' is 'figurational processes' or just 'process analysis' while Blumer (1969) has spoken of 'joint activity' as the conceptual key which obviates the need for a dualism or dualistic thinking.

The analysis of interpersonal control presented in this book takes a very different view of the most appropriate way of dealing with the agency–structure problem. Those who have proposed 'replacement' conceptual singularities have effectively dispossessed social reality of some of its essential domains. This strategy is quite inadequate for very simple, but massively important reasons. As in cosmology, 'singularities' are the centres of black holes. And like black holes in the physical universe, conceptual singularities as applied to the social universe absorb and destroy everything around them. The argument that the social world can be represented by conceptual singularities means that the black holes that surround them 'eat up' large chunks of social reality and leave us with a severely impoverished, emptied-out vision of the social world.

Rebuilding the Social Universe

A reversal of this reductive process is urgently needed. Instead of narrowing down our understanding of social reality by insisting that it can be represented and explained by singular unifying principles, we need to unpack and open up the explanatory range and power of social analysis. This can only be accomplished by identifying the elements forming the variegated, layered and multi-dimensional nature of social reality. In short, we must veer away from the reductive force of singularities and adopt a more expansive and inclusive view of the social universe.

This project should begin with unpacking the two main terms of the agency–structure problem rather than leaving them as either a simple dualism, or by assuming that they are seamlessly joined. By doing the latter, we lose analytic grip on the distinctive characteristics of social reality to which the two terms refer. Instead, we need to examine more closely what we mean by both agency and structure in order to expand our understanding of them. We must envision them as important aspects of a richly textured social world (reality). Once we put them under the microscope, so to speak, we find that they are in dire need of revision. What has been assumed about their ontological dimensions and explanatory importance needs drastic upgrading.

Social Agency and Psychobiography

The concept of 'social agency' (and its twin 'social action') suffers considerably by being stretched to cover an extremely diverse range of phenomena. This has led to ambiguity about what exactly the term refers to, and to a distorted view of the nature of human being and doing. In particular, the term compacts two very distinct features of human social behaviour that are urgently in need of independent reconstruction. First, the rather naïve assumption that the term 'social agency' says anything meaningful about the capacities of particular individuals or their social behaviour needs to be questioned.

In this sense, the term 'social agency' has been used to imply that an essential characteristic of all human beings is their transformative capacity (Giddens 1984) – in other words, being able to deal with life, make decisions, make a difference to your life. But this is a misleadingly unqualified assertion. In so far as this notion of social agency may serve as an important (although essentially crude) counter to the view that human beings are simply helpless and hapless victims of social forces, there is a grain of truth in this. But it is a case of one crude approximation being replaced by another.

It fails to register an appreciation of the variable capacities – or 'powers' – possessed by individuals. But we should also go on to distinguish between an individual's powers deriving from 'inner potential' (such as self-confidence, self-esteem, resilience) and those that represent restrictions or enlargements impressed on them by the social environment (for example, how self-confidence might be diminished by the experience of failure). This is not to set up a radical or 'artificial' division between 'external' and 'internal', it is merely to indicate that there are crucially important differences to do with the locus of individual powers that must not be overlooked.

The failure to make this distinction (or the wilful attempt to break it down) has been the bane of those sociologists intent on making the social world an exclusively social construct. Unfortunately it results in an impoverished view of both society and human beings. It also leaves sociology unable to conceive of individuals as uniquely variable in their capacities and powers. Hence it becomes a stumbling block to an adequate understanding of the links between subjective and social reality.

The concept of 'psychobiography' embraces the unique subjective configuration of emotional-cognitive capacities acquired by individuals during the course of their personal and social development. But it also indicates the variability of such powers in relation to different phases of their lives and social involvements. In this respect social settings and contexts are very important influences upon individual powers and capacities. However, they must not be confused with, absorb, or dissolve the distinctive nature of the inner, subjective life of human beings. In this sense to speak of human agency or transformative capacity (a generic capacity to alter one's social circumstances) tells us little, if anything, about real people or real individuals. Human beings do not have *generic* human or social qualities. Beyond the purely artificial confines of abstract philosophical discussion, there are no such things as human beings in general. There are only (unique) individuals, uniquely formed in the more generalized contexts of social environments.

These considerations are germane to a proper understanding of interpersonal control. While interpersonal activity is irreducibly social in nature, it is formed and shaped from the concerted activity of individuals. Inner subjective powers and capacities must not be lost in the rush to emphasize the influence of social forces (inter-subjective or otherwise). At the same time it is pointless to argue that individuals operate outside these social influences, or to deny that social forces sometimes override the 'free play' of subjective capacities and processes.

We need to be able to account for the fact that some people are more confident of, or in tune with, themselves than others and hence are more capable of managing social situations. They exert more subjective power, and thus control, over their circumstances. On the other hand, we need to register that other individuals, perhaps because of a 'learned helplessness' (or some other psychological debilitation), are less effective in dealing with desperate circumstances or the 'ordinary' misfortunes of life. It is misleading to speak of transformative power as a generic capacity – as if everyone had equivalent powers and possibilities for control. They don't, and that's what makes them unique in the first place.

Agency and Situated Activity

We must be careful to distinguish between, on the one hand, personal control stemming from individual agency and, on the other, control as an aspect of social interaction. A person's ability to control and influence others is conditioned by the unfolding nature of social interaction. An individual's powers – say their self-confidence or their ability to get on well with others – may be reined in or enhanced as an effect of the social interaction, for example by incurring the disapproval of the others.

This issue runs parallel to the idea that individuals have generic powers. It is necessary to disentangle generic features of social interaction from the detailed circumstances associated with *actual* encounters. It is true, as Mead (1967) and others have shown, that general processes such as symbolic exchange and the creation of meaning are present in social interaction. However, what is actually 'done' or accomplished by those involved in specific instances of interaction involves a different set of issues.

For an observer to understand real behaviour in real time, he or she must possess 'inside' knowledge (from within the situation); it cannot be read off from prior knowledge or external observation. In this sense the meaning of behaviour – fuelled, for example, by drugs, or prompted by an argument between friends – is closely associated with the actual situations in which they occur and the particular people involved. As ethnomethodologists and phenomenologists have observed, inevitably the meaning of such behaviour will be imbued with a local flavour. However, the unique and local flavour of behaviour that flows from these meanings does not arise simply because they are tied to unique blends of intersubjectivity (as phenomenologists insist). Rather, it is because situated activity is a point of confluence for the influence of different but overlapping social domains. Thus situated activity mediates the influences of individuals as well as the settings and contexts of their activities. It is unique because it is a unique blend of social domain influences, not because it stems from a unitary source.

Self-identity, Emotion and Agency

To a considerable extent, human social agency is the property of a person and, therefore, is closely linked to their other particular characteristics. But this is often forgotten in discussions that speak of agency as if it were generic capacity (or even, as a reflex of social discourses). Agency cannot be understood without reference to a person's self-identity and their emotional and psychological make-up. In this respect, much human behaviour is motivated around emotional needs, such as love, approval, a sense of worth and so on. We are all enmeshed in the reciprocal satisfaction of each other's needs – a process that entails both self-control and control over others. But these are not smooth-flowing, problem-free processes. Satisfying one's own and other's needs at the same time requires a 'balancing act' fraught with highly charged feelings, sometimes accompanied by cataclysmic emotional eruptions.

A person may set out with the best of intentions but lack any real awareness of the actual impact of their behaviour on another person. This may result in hurt feelings all-round, as when the over-protective behaviour of a parent has the inadvertent effect of humiliating their son or daughter, or where a person arranges a surprise party for a friend but only succeeds in embarrassing them because they don't like surprises. In short, even if the best interests of all the participants are borne in mind during such emotional exchanges, there is no guarantee that shared satisfaction will result. Such a state of affairs may be achieved only with the utmost delicacy, expertise and flair. That this is actually accomplished on a fairly regular, everyday basis (even if only 'approximately') is a great testament to the skills and ingenuity of most people.

The brilliance of this mutual accomplishment is further highlighted by the fact that it is achieved directly in the face of 'a fast moving blur of misunderstanding, error, folly, and alienation, with only rare and all too brief moments of attunement', which Scheff (1990: 50) suggests is our typical experience of encounters. In this sense it is more a matter of making the best of a difficult task beset by all manner of unpredictable dangers. Of course, none of us has much option. It's the only way in which we can safeguard our social inclusion, involvement or emotional satisfaction.

In the ordinary encounters of everyday life we need to reaffirm our sense of ourselves as competent and efficacious actors. Any diminution of this felt sense would sabotage our efforts to carry through, or carry on with our active engagements with others. But to reiterate, this is an inherently emotional enterprise involving the unique personal qualities, needs and predispositions of individuals. In this sense we must reject Goffman's view of emotion as existing 'not within the individual but within the social system' (1967: 108).

The view of emotion adopted here has much more in common with Scheff (1990) and Hochschild (1984). They have suggested that a viable treatment of emotion in social interaction must go well beyond the confines of what Goffman refers to as the 'syntactic relations among the acts of different persons mutually present to one another' (1967: 2–3). The 'individual and his psychology' must be incorporated into any analysis of social encounters, if it is to have any adequate explanatory bite at all. In particular, Hochschild's view of the study of emotion as necessarily drawing on psychological, interactional and social-structural domains avoids the conceptual singularities and black holes implicit in social constructionism.

Agency and Interpersonal Control

Although 'social agency' has always been about individual power and control, issues of interpersonal control are rarely broached in this context. Since much social behaviour is motivated around emotional need and self-competence, it is not surprising that these forces greatly infuse behaviour with purpose and direction. But what are the objects of this energy? General discussions of agency have left this question unanswered. The importance of the impulse and general orientation to control are paramount here. In this respect there are three main areas or objects of controlling concern; the self as object of its own control, other people, and the individual's current life situation.

Through self-control, individuals attempt to master (or at least competently deal with) their social world. To know oneself, to be 'roughly' in charge of one's emotional responses, is necessary in order to win influence and exert control in the wider social world. The ability to influence others and control them 'benignly' depends on being able to 'read' their feelings, and respond to them in a way that creates mutual satisfaction. Benign control is ubiquitous in social life and is an inherent feature of all social interaction. It is further distinguished from other kinds of control by its connection with co-operation and altruism and its concern with others' interests and feelings. Thus it is quite unlike exploitative forms of control which rely on suppressing the victim's or target's needs, interests and feelings in favour of the perpetrator's. But benign and exploitative control are ranged along a continuum, from the generic and 'healthy' benign control at one end, to pathological types exemplified by domination and exploitation at the other (see Chapter 5).

The final 'object' of a person's controlling concerns is his or her wider life situation, which draws together a number of overlapping life sectors (work, leisure, private life and so on) and reflects their overall position of control. It is a sensitive indicator of mental well-being as well as an expression of the current 'state' of the control balance. The common focus of these possible objects of control is the individual's dependence on them for the fulfilment or satisfaction of needs, concerns and problems. It is crucial not to think of agency as an open-ended and 'abstract' capacity. Social agency never remains diffuse or undirected; it is always locked into the pragmatics of interpersonal control and is driven by individual and social requirements.

Social Settings and Interpersonal Behaviour

What 'structure' refers to in the couplet 'agency–structure' also needs unpacking to reveal the complex social reality it obscures. The trouble is that the term enforces a compaction of social phenomena and this simply adds to the problems caused by attempts to reduce agency–structure relations to some unifying principle. Thus the immediate setting of situated activity must be understood as a distinctive domain of social reality with its own characteristics and properties.

Social interaction is never simply a free creation of individuals – it is always influenced by the social environment – and social settings are the most 'immediate' (that is, closest to the action) features of this environment. They represent already constructed arenas of social behaviour. Social settings are organized social relations that embody distinctive rules and expectations about the behaviour that takes place within their confines. The more visible and sharply defined of these settings are those possessing a clear, physically demarcated and crystallized form, as found in many organizations such as factories, hospitals, schools, universities, military and police establishments, hospices, and so on. Such settings are aggregations of defined positions, relations and social practices that significantly influence the behaviour of those operating within them.

Less formalized and dispersed settings like family and friendship networks, or those involving sexual or emotional intimacy, are more loosely defined in terms of the kinds of relationships, positions and practices they co-ordinate or bring together. However, in terms of their effects on behaviour, they are no less influential. Social settings represent the most immediate layering of social structure that wraps around individuals and their social relationships.

Wider Structural or System Features

Unpacking the term 'structure' still further, it is also necessary to distinguish between settings as the most adjacent to social behaviour as compared with more removed and impersonal aspects. Thus social settings are very different kinds of phenomena to society-wide divisions of class, gender and ethnicity. In turn these differ in form to cultural, discursive, linguistic and symbolic phenomena such as the mass media – films, TV, video, the internet, advertisements, magazines, newspapers, and so on. What they have in common is their continually reproduced nature as institutionalized features of society. However, they differ in terms of their proximity to behaviour, the extent of their local influence over it, and the actual form they take as features of social reality.

Interpersonal control is influenced in different ways by different systemic (or 'structural') features. Thus it is important to distinguish between them, especially since their differences are obscured by the blanket term 'structure'. This is surely the only way in which their differential effects on social behaviour and interpersonal relations can be reliably assessed.

The Dual Nature of Social Relations

The view that social 'relations' or 'relationships' have a singular nature is misleading. Social behaviour arises in the interplay between the creative inputs of individuals and the pre-existing social resources they draw upon to help them formulate their behaviour. This interplay can be seen in the example of language and language use. We draw upon and generally conform to grammatical and syntactical rules and vocabulary items in order to make ourselves understandable to others in everyday talk and conversation. But at the same time as drawing upon these resources, we also produce sentences and communicate meanings that are novel in the sense that they convey our own interpretations and viewpoints.

This interplay between creativity and conformity is also mirrored in the facilitating or enabling function of linguistic resources as compared with their constraining nature. That is, linguistic rules make it possible for us to say certain things and to communicate with others, while at the same time these rules limit what counts as correct or understandable utterances. That social relationships also straddle this divide is directly expressed in the tension between innovative and reproduced aspects of social relations.

In social interaction there is an inevitable push towards 'innovation' in terms of producing novel meanings and solutions posed by the immediate situation and those involved in it. For example, a group of people might meet for a drink before deciding what they will do for the rest of the evening. Each individual will contribute (even if only negatively by refusing to have an opinion) to making this decision. Each one might have his or her own very different ideas about how the evening should be spent. So in part the innovation is the result of each individual bringing his or her own unique resources and contributing to the encounter in a distinctive manner.

However, the push towards innovation is also a consequence of the collective 'flow' and emergent outcomes of encounters. Thus, although each individual may have their own ideas about how to spend the evening, collectively the group has to come up with a decision that suits everybody to some degree. Thus individual preferences may have to take a back-seat to the will of the majority. In so doing, the group will come up with a generally 'agreed' decision that broadly fits with everyone's preferences. In this sense the line of action that was agreed was an emergent feature of the encounter itself.

But innovation in interaction is counterbalanced by the tendency to rely on precedent as a means of guiding and informing current behaviour. Searching for relevant precedent means consulting a bank of prior experience and memory traces that may contain clues, recipes and behavioural solutions applicable to the current situation. In practical terms the individual says to him or herself, 'Have I met this situation before?' And, if so, how did I deal with it? Did my response lead to a successful outcome? Do I need to modify my response to take account of changed circumstances? In this respect, searching for a precedent in terms of past experience furnishes us with a template against which current experience may be evaluated.

From the point of view of society (social system, social structure), precedent is more or less deeply embedded in its traditions, customs, habits, values, expectations, institutionalized over social time and space. Precedent is an essential part of the reproduced character of society as it has been established, and continues to be reaffirmed through everyday routines, such as going to the pub, hobbies, sports and other leisure activities, ceremonies such as weddings and graduations, rituals of courtship and friendship, obligations to family ties, and so on.

The dual nature of social relations then, is reflected in the tension between their reproduced character (the extent of their cultural power, importance and sedimentation in time) and the human tendency to forge novel solutions to interactive problems in the ebb and flow of social encounters. In this sense all kinds of social relationships embody both these tendencies, although the exact mix or balance between them varies according to the kind of social setting in which they occur. For example, depending on their setting, social relations vary in the extent to which they constrain and shape social behaviour and their 'tolerance' for innovative behaviour. Commentators (notably Turner 1962 and Stryker 1981) have pointed out that in intimate, primary or private spheres of life (for example, personal or intimate relationships) there is greater latitude for appropriate or tolerated behaviour. In these more 'liberal' settings, people are freer to interpret behavioural requirements whereas in more formal and restrictive settings (such as schools, work, police and religious organizations), closer conformity to 'established' practices is required.

The Social Sources of Power

Power is everywhere, as Foucault (1980) has remarked. However, the form of power is not everywhere the same, a crucial qualification omitted by Foucault. But emotion is also a constant companion of power – a proposition consistent with the work of Kemper (1978), Collins (1983), Hochschild (1983) and Barbalet (2001). The idea that power and emotion are everywhere found together gets to the heart of the issue. Power is not the special preserve of the 'movers and shakers' of the world, nor can it be regarded as something closeted away and 'revealed' only on special occasions. It saturates our very being and existence as actors whoever and wherever we are in the social world. And so, along with a model of social life as multi-dimensional, complex and variegated, we must add a complementary view of power.

Thinking of power as uni-dimensional must be resisted. Theorists and social analysts have regularly succumbed to the idea that power can be encapsulated in a unitary definition. But to understand its influence on interpersonal control, it is necessary to recognize the multi-faceted nature of power. Thus power must be construed as an amalgam of influences – individual, interpersonal, positional, discursive-practical, social-structural (or systemic) and symbolic. It is a confluent mixture of these divergent influences and points of origin.

Creativity and Constraint in Social Life

Those who view agency and structure as a seamlessly unified singularity also tend to overstate the socially creative capacities of human beings. They argue that we simultaneously create and recreate ('produce and reproduce', 'constitute and reconstitute') society in each and every instance of social behaviour. But this is a misleadingly generous view of the impact and creativity of routine behaviour on society as a whole. At the same time, and paradoxically, such a view underestimates the extent of localized creativity of people in their situated activities.

It is true to say that most examples of social activity have 'reproductive effects', in so far as the employment of social rules and resources automatically reproduces and reaffirms them over time. Thus, for example, each time we chat or converse with others, we inadvertently reproduce the rules, conventions and rituals of communication and language use. However, there is here little in the way of genuine or 'important' creativity.

In everyday routines we do not 'create' society or invent new rules of speech, or novel ways of doing things. We largely repeat, re-apply and reaffirm what already exists and is available to us.

Thus most of our (routine) everyday behaviour is socially reproductive, while our wider creative contribution is minimal. On the other hand, situated activity encourages local creativity in which everyday encounters produce transient but creative outcomes. Thus, as in a previous example, a group of friends who meet early to decide what to do during the rest of the evening will produce an emergent, creative outcome in their collective endeavour of deciding what to do. But it is crucial to get such creativity in perspective, in the sense that it has limited implications for the wider society. Of course, much of what may be described as creative is regarded as real and consequential for those involved. But the influence of these creations remains restricted to those who are party to the proceedings – whose 'involvement', as Goffman would say, has been 'ratified'.

With the dispersal of these participants, the reality created through their presence also disappears. Even when in subsequent encounters there is a carry-over of business or proceedings, the 'shared' reality is limited to those specifically involved. While many such shared experiences may be thrilling and life-changing for the participants (meeting a romantic partner, participating in an exciting activity), they remain quite inconsequential for the wider world. To a large extent, interpersonal relations have local elements attaching to them. The participants bring their unique personal qualities to bear on proceedings, while their purposes are unravelled and played out in very specific circumstances. In that sense those involved are caught up in an enterprise wholly constructed from their mutual dealings.

At the same time, however, the types of control and the strategies employed in order to create such local realities are themselves reproduced social practices. Thus the types of interpersonal control, control strategies, settings and typical forms of emotional expression are more than ephemeral, local versions of social reality. They represent the reproduced social practices that serve as templates for the construction of local realities.

The Interaction Order

Erving Goffman's notion of 'the interaction order' has been 'appropriated' in different ways by theorists from different perspectives. Although there are substantial disagreements as to its theoretical importance, the debate surrounding the interaction order holds an important, albeit partial, key to the analysis of interpersonal relations. That is to say, it can supply but one part of a far more complicated story.

What does Goffman mean by 'the interaction order'? In his most systematic discussion of it (1983) he suggests that it refers to a domain (of interaction) in its own right, which is different from, but closely related to, and influenced by the wider institutional order. It involves a cluster of issues, the first of which is the care and maintenance of the social self. Thus the interaction order enables us to deal with the sorts of problems we face in attempting to project certain images of ourselves in public. In this respect there are mutual moral obligations that bind us with others over the question of self-care. Although the manipulation of others and the violation of their self-integrity do occur, these tendencies are balanced by a morally informed attitude of trust, tact and respect for one another. Although altruism plays a part here, interaction itself involves a level of co-operation that can be cannot be sustained without at least some mutual trust and respect. Thus, for example, when in interaction a person loses face (or is threatened with it), a typical response is for others to remedy the situation so that it does not happen or so that its damaging consequences to a person's self-esteem and social poise are minimized.

In this sense the interaction order depends on people's adherence to generally unspoken 'rules' about what is right and what feels OK in encounters. Such rules suggest that we should display a certain level of involvement when engaged with others. For example, when we are intimately engaged with another, we shouldn't be distracted by side-interests such as watching TV or checking the sports results. In encounters we should act with propriety and not violate the hidden assumptions about appropriate behaviour. When passing others on the street, we should display civil inattention towards them – that is, not stare too much or intrude upon their privacy or anonymity.

Goffman's point is that it is the interaction order itself that deals with the sensitivities and subtleties of appropriate behaviour between ourselves and others who are in our 'response presence', as he phrases it. This is not handled primarily by the institutional order, although Goffman envisages the relationship between the interaction order and the institutional order as ultimately based on a 'loose-coupling' arrangement. But Goffman's views on the nature of the interaction order have become surrounded by disagreements as to its theoretical importance. Consequently, Goffman's original vision needs to be rescued from the misleading confusions associated with two subsequent interpretations.

Although Goffman thought of social reality in general as comprising two relatively independent but 'loosely coupled' social orders (the 'institutional order' and the 'interaction order'), this looks much like a standard version of the action–structure problem. It is not really surprising, therefore, that Giddens (1987) objects to the very idea of an interaction order in its own right, largely independent of institutional phenomena. This is because the standard view of agency–structure is at odds with

Giddens's determination to rid social analysis of (what he takes to be) false dualisms. Giddens implies that the agency–structure distinction is made redundant by his concept of the 'duality of structure' because it apparently synthesizes (but actually dissolves) agency and structure into one seamless unity. For Giddens, there is no independent (or relatively autonomous) order of social interaction. All that exists is the simultaneous production and reproduction of social practices via the duality of structure.

But Goffman's notion of a loose coupling of institutional and interactional orders has much greater explanatory scope. The idea of a relatively autonomous interaction order more adequately addresses the manner in which interactive processes mediate the effects of institutional phenomena. A 'duality of structure' cannot do this because it simply collapses agency and structure together without any (independent) mediation by situated activity.

Rawls's (1987) quite opposite interpretation of the interaction order is in line with the views of symbolic interactionists, ethnomethodologists and phenomenologists, who insist on the more or less complete autonomy of the interaction order. Rawls expresses this most clearly by insisting that the major defining features of the interaction order are internally managed and constituted by that order. From this viewpoint the idea that institutional features are anything more than an inert backdrop to the 'real business' of social life is regarded as anathema. But this is quite at odds with Goffman's view of the importance of the institutional order and its loosely coupled relationship with the interaction order. Although departing from Goffman in this respect, at the same time these same authors endorse his dismissal of individual psychology in the constitution of interaction. Thus this approach adopts a vision of the interaction order as internally ordered, self-sufficient and, hence, independent of any other domain of social reality.

On the surface this position is different from that of Giddens. The 'duality of structure' is replaced by the notion of self-ordered interaction processes. However, if we stray below the surface the overall strategy is similar, involving the reduction of a complex, variegated, social reality to an ontological singularity. Again it highlights a radical departure from Goffman's dualistic vision. Both Giddens's and Rawls's strategies remove the subtlety and complexity from Goffman's vision of the loose coupling between institutional and interaction orders. In the light of these (mis)interpretations, it is essential to reinstate Goffman's actual position if the concept of the interaction order is to have any useful or worthwhile place in social analysis. Certainly from the point of view of providing an adequate account of interpersonal control, the idea of a *relatively autonomous* domain of social reality is crucial. But this cannot be at the expense of removing the complexity and multi-faceted character of social reality.

The Interaction Order: a Confusion and Conflation

Goffman's understanding of the interaction order is too elastic. It embraces too much. In the process it fails to distinguish between the creative elements of situated activity and the reproduced aspects of social systems. It also generates confusion. On the one hand, Goffman highlights the importance of the 'arrivals and departures' of those involved as the principal defining features of what he variously terms 'encounters', 'focused gatherings' or 'situated activity'. In this respect he emphasizes the evanescent quality of local social realities in which people decide how they will interpret rules and create meaning, say about the extent to which they will display involvement or respect or trust other individuals.

On the other hand, Goffman also speaks of the interaction order as sets of (reproduced) rules and expectations that apply to social interaction in general, such as involvement obligations, situational propriety, civil inattention, trust, accessibility and so on (Manning 1992). But by failing to distinguish between encounters themselves and the rules and resources on which people draw in making encounters happen, Goffman overlooks the very different ontological characteristics of these phenomena. He then compounds the mistake by assuming that these elements are all similar because they all 'belong' to the interaction order.

Later commentators have repeated Goffman's error here and this has led to the two opposed accounts of the role and importance of the interaction order. Giddens's account emphasizes the general institutional and cultural nature of rules about trust and involvement and so on, and suggests that there is no need for the 'extra' concept of an interaction order. Thus Giddens complains that Goffman unnecessarily restricts these phenomena (trust, involvement obligations and so on) to the interaction order itself, whereas, in fact, they also belong to the wider institutional context.

Giddens is correct to insist that such phenomena do not belong exclusively to an interaction order in its own right. However, at the same time, he completely misses the ontological distinctiveness of situated activity as the localized 'delivery system' of social behaviour. Hence he overlooks the relative autonomy of situated activity and its important mediating influence on social behaviour. In direct contrast to Giddens, Rawls and others (see Malone 1997) have focused on precisely those aspects of the interaction order that Goffman deals with as the 'internal' properties of situated activity (local interpretations or rules and meanings) which are reflected in, and punctuated by, the arrivals and departures of ratified participants. Unfortunately this interpretation of the interaction order has the converse effect of ignoring its constitutive links with a wider cultural, discursive and institutional order, of which involvements, obligations, trust and so on are an integral part.

The only viable way out of this impasse is to acknowledge the ontological (and explanatory) distinction between situated activity and aspects of the cultural and institutional order. By so doing we preserve the situation-specific, localized nature of real episodes of interaction, but also accept that this domain of social reality is not insulated from wider systemic influences. The boundaries between domains are permeable and allow for the mutual interchange of influences and effects. Importantly, the distinction allows us to appreciate the pivotal role of situated activity as a conduit and relay between individuals and their wider social entanglements.

The Theory of Interpersonal Control

Any theory or analysis of interpersonal control must be based on the assumption that it is grounded in ontologically distinct domains of social reality. We must resist the temptation to oversimplify social reality by narrowing its scope to a singular domain and by attempting to explain social behaviour by exclusive reference to it. Thus situated activity must be viewed as one of several interconnected and relatively autonomous domains. We cannot grasp the true nature of interpersonal control if we see it as the generalized expression of all-encompassing social influences. A refusal to acknowledge the relative autonomy of individuals (psychobiography) or situated activity simply reproduces the worst excesses of an unfettered social constructionism or determinism. Equally, to understand 'structures' or 'systems' (including discourses) as if they were expressions of a uniform social reality is to simplify and denature that reality.

An adequate analysis of interpersonal control necessitates that the standard formulation of the agency–structure problem must undergo some radical revision. Generally the relationship must be seen in more textured, variegated and complex terms. Attempts to contain it within a simple dualism (agency–structure) or to reduce it to some conceptual and ontological singularity ('discursive practices', 'duality of structure, intersubjectivity, the interaction order) are over-simplifications of very complex social processes.

The drawback of collapsing the constituent elements of social reality together into a supposedly seamless union is that we lose explanatory hold on many of the most important and distinctive properties of social reality.

Summary

- Both terms of the agency–structure couplet need to be unpacked in order to understand interpersonal control.
- Agency needs to register variations in competence and efficacy produced by differences in individual psychobiographies as well as the influence of identity issues involving emotion and self-esteem.
- The concept of structure (or system) needs to be unpacked to take account of settings and wider contextual resources that influence interpersonal control.
- It is also necessary to understand the dual nature of social relations and the importance of different forms of power as they derive from different social domains.
- The nature and limitations of individual creativity must be seen in a realistic light and in the context of differing domains of social reality.
- While it is insightful in certain respects, Goffman's concept of the interaction order requires amendment in order to properly account for interpersonal control.

2

The Psychology of Personal Control

Preview

- Emotional needs and issues around self-identity and threats to basic security in everyday life.
- The self as executive centre and social agent.
- Psycho-social development of personal control.
- Benign control and its association with avoiding helplessness; the tensions between separateness and relatedness; emotional intelligence; personal appeals; negative celebrity; personal significance.
- The need for personal control in social life.
- The links between self and society.

We need to understand the 'psychology' of the person before we can fully grasp the dynamic relationship between interpersonal control, emotion and self-identity. The intertwining influences of emotion, control and self-identity feed directly into the transactions of everyday social interaction via the psychological dispositions of the individual.

Emotion and Self-identity

Although emotion and control are closely bound together, it is necessary to examine them separately. Doing so will expose the unique contribution that each makes to the other when they are combined. Neither emotion nor control is more basic or important. Emotion underlies control just as control underlies emotion. Both statements are true as far as self-identity is concerned. To say that the self has an emotional nature is to lay claim to the view that we are not simply cold, logical and reasoning beings. The self is not emptily 'aware' of its surrounding world; in fact, 'awareness' is always located in some mood or attitude directed towards whatever it contemplates. Thus the idea that 'reflective awareness' and self-monitoring are the most important human characteristics (Giddens 1984) falls rather short of the mark. Possessing reflective awareness says little about the content of awareness or how it is employed.

Although there is no doubt that people often act reasonably and are capable of rational decision-making, they never do so in the complete absence of emotion. Even what may seem purely practical tasks are generally replete with emotional freight. Routine chores like mowing the lawn or washing dishes are performed under the direct influence of prevailing moods, attitudes and feelings. Onerous tasks are typically tackled in ways that express boredom, enthusiasm or irritability. For example, they may be an unwelcome distraction from what might be considered more important or urgent matters (such as the state of your most intimate relationship, your son's illness or your impending retirement).

Even where emotions are not part of the task itself, feelings always intrude into the flow of awareness, affecting your mood and attitude. If this is so when doing things that have no apparent or obvious connection with feelings, our general human dealings are obviously more fertile ground for the influence of moods, feelings and emotional attitudes. Relationships involve the interchange of emotional attitudes and dispositions, often creating a complex knot of emotional currents and energies running through them.

The Self and Basic Security

Why do emotions play such a diffuse part in our self-identities and social conduct? It is best to approach this question by first understanding the self as a finely tuned security system – with an executive centre. The continuity of a person's self and their sense of identity as a healthy, integrated being is entirely dependent on his or her emotional needs being validated, given support and satisfied. If there is not enough validation and support for emotional needs, then a person's self-esteem and self-confidence will suffer and deteriorate.

Continuing psychological health depends upon a robust self-security system. That is, one in which the person receives enough emotional validation and support to ensure that the basic self system can withstand any threats to it. These 'threats' could be internal in the sense that a fragile balance of emotional forces may fall into an even more dangerous state of disrepair. For example, self-doubt and second thoughts generated by thwarted ambition may produce a loss of basic confidence and self-belief.

On the other hand there are important external threats. Everyday encounters are not as smooth as they often appear. The tendency of certain individuals to undermine others or 'put them in their place' is a common example highlighting the vulnerabilities of the self. But even those seemingly benign routine circumstances that take up the greater part of everyday life are also emotionally complex. This can be observed in the simplest conversations and interactions, where the participants shift and shape themselves in relation to the unfolding of the encounter. This is illustrated in the way in which we 'jockey' for conversational space, receive compliments, react to disapproval, and then deliberately formulate our behaviour in accordance with these signals.

We are aware of our own status and power as compared with those with whom we interact and what this means for the way in which we respond to them. We constantly monitor our own and others' behaviour in an effort to find a clear direction and strategy for future behaviour. We need to be able to read each other's behaviour in order to know what's in store a little further on in the encounter. We need to able to repair any damage we've done in the form of apologies or promises. Having sensitivity and insight in the search for these clues allows us to perform difficult social 'operations' such as helping ourselves or someone else, to maintain or retrieve dignity through face-saving rituals.

In these different ways the self is vulnerable to routine pitfalls and pummelings that are the elemental stuff of everyday encounters. This requires us to be vigilant enough to protect ourselves against such incursions lest they undermine self-confidence and self-esteem. We shore ourselves up against the possibility of negative responses from others by putting on appearances, or by pretending not to have heard, and so on. However, these protective devices will amount to little if you are already uncertain or doubt your abilities in the first place. If you are hungry for validation and psychological support, then you will be even more susceptible to any further loss of emotional energy, self-worth and self-esteem.

The basic security system is a network of social and psychological processes and is the bedrock of the self and personal identity. As long as this system remains in a fair state of balance – such that a person's emotional and other needs are being met – then the self will remain strong and adequately supported. But how is this complex of diverse feeling tones, turbulences and energies orchestrated?

The Self as Executive Centre and Social Agent

First the self is not only a centre of awareness in which emotional needs compete for attention, but it is also an executive centre. That is, it is the point at which the individual arranges such needs in some order of priority as a prelude to formulating and shaping his or her behaviour. This is achieved within the parameters set by the individual's innate capacities and unfolding life situation. In this sense the self is the point of origin of action.

This executive self creates relative order out of the potential chaos of feeling responses that threaten to swamp action and bog it down. As agent of its own action, the self must sort these emotional-need claims into a queue that is perpetually on the point of disorder but always drawing back from it. Practically, we reason that so and so 'is my most pressing problem, so I'll tackle this first [say patch up a quarrel with an elderly parent] and then I'll be able to concentrate on getting them to move to a safer neighbourhood'.

Having once prioritized the need claims, the self must also precipitate the action. It must order the claims into a series of action plans based on gathered evidence and stored experience. The successful implementation of action plans has the effect of draining tension from the emotional security system. For example, if you patch up the quarrel with your parent and then persuade them to live in a safer neighbourhood, many psychological issues and demands will be alleviated. Simultaneously, however, other problems will be promoted to the front of the queue and fill the vacant space. Thus, for example, this will allow you to devote time and space to 'repairing' your relationship with your partner.

This is not accomplished in a slow and plodding manner as if the self simply adopted the most rational plan available and executed it perfectly in all its detail. The decision-making process is much messier and less definitive than the unfolding of a carefully worked plan. Executive decisions are just as emotionally infused as any other area of the self and behaviour, therefore they don't necessarily slavishly follow a plan in an objective manner. Thus executive decisions are informed by the subjective logic of a person's lived reality – the way the world appears from subjective experience. The efficacy of such decisions must be judged in terms of the actor's viewpoint and not that of an external observer. What appears to be rational from one person's point of view may not be so from another's.

It is because human beings are naturally active and inquisitive that the self is a centre of 'doing' (as well as being). The self is oriented to control (of others) in order to create behavioural solutions to practical problems. That is, answers to questions of how to act or respond in a manner that will alleviate the pressures of emotional needs and social and psychological demands.

The Psycho-social Development of Control

The self and processes of control exist within a social field – a changing network of social relationships and a constantly unfolding life situation.

From the outset the individual's possession of and urge to use skills associated with interpersonal control are already at a premium. These tendencies are exemplified in the psycho-social development of the human infant as detailed by Piaget. In order for a baby to develop into a competent adult, he or she has to explore the world around them and learn essential skills to manipulate it in a way that allows them to participate meaningfully in that environment.

The baby not only has to understand the principles that underpin their environment but also has to make an impression on their physical and social circumstances. They must have some understanding of how things work in order to alter this world in a manner that satisfies them and helps to motivate further exploratory activity. For example, making an object such as a rattle or a doll move, or being successful in capturing the attention of a parent, has in-built reinforcements for such exploratory behaviour. The more physical and emotional rewards that accrue from such attempts to manipulate the world, the more likely are they to step up the exploratory activity.

The point is that the child's relation to the world is already one in which control and manipulation are central and defining elements. Crucially, learning how to manipulate people by using relevant strategies at appropriate stages of maturation (sensory-motor, concrete operations and formal operations) is the principal means by which the child develops and matures intellectually as well as socially. In this elemental sense it could be said that learning to be a competent human being integrally involves acquiring the skills of social manipulation.

In the first instance these manipulative skills are such that the interests of both parties are catered for and both get something of value out of the transaction. For example, by crying the child gets some food while in return, the parent gets a happy and therefore much less demanding baby. Learning moral rules of behaviour, manners, appropriate forms of pressure, and other requirements of social convention simply reinforces this tendency. However, it is also likely that the child will eventually have some experiential exposure to more exploitative control strategies. Since the child's whole emotional and psychological satisfaction and mental well-being depends on the ability to manipulatively transact with the social world, it is more than likely that the child will experiment with these more exploitative forms. However, at some point the child will be confronted with the idea of the moral wrongness and social inappropriateness of basing its whole modus operandi around the self-interested exploitation of others.

It is obviously socially desirable that the child does not simply opt wholesale for exploitative control. Whether or not the child eventually bases its self-identity predominantly around exploitative, as opposed to benign, control strategies depends on several variables. These include the extent to which the parents themselves utilize and generally emphasize exploitative control in their own transactions with the child and the child's subsequent life experiences and problems. Of course, the basic social division engendered by the different self-identity options here concerns that between social and anti-social behaviour. At one extreme, anti-social behaviour may include simply being difficult to get on with, or being obstructive. The use of psychological terror tactics or emotional blackmail to get what you want represents a ratcheting-up of control intensity.

At the other end of the continuum are extreme forms of domination – violence, rape, murder and so on – that don't concern us at this juncture. That they are part of a graded continuum is, however, important for understanding the connections between very different forms of human behaviour. For current purposes, the fact that many of the more 'moderate' forms of exploitative control – such as emotional blackmail – are commonly employed in everyday social encounters is of more relevance. They represent the limit of what might be termed socially 'acceptable' ('tolerated' might be a better word) kinds of exploitation.

Let us for the moment suppose that our young adult adopts a fairly pro-social line as far as his or her own personal identity is concerned. That is, whilst not being averse to the occasional use of 'milder' types of emotional blackmail (perhaps on some friends and family members), this individual mostly adopts benign forms of control and influence. What exactly is entailed in benign control?

Personal Mastery and Benign Control

'Mastery' should here be understood in a positive sense that limits it to the sphere of personal effectiveness. Thus our young adult will 'master' her environment in so far as she feels satisfied about the level of control she has over her life. In social life in particular, the ability to 'make a difference' is crucial to an individual's sense of competent personhood. Such a healthy self (what Becker (1974), calls a positive locus of value), is the executive centre responsible for the initiation and co-ordination of behaviour geared to the accomplishment of emotional satisfaction.

This, in itself, is a control issue that centres on the ability to create relationships that are psychologically and emotionally fulfilling, and which greatly contribute to the creation of both a fairly stable, but at the same time evolving, universe of meaning for the person. Thus the ability to initiate and maintain meaningful relationships at different levels of intimacy is essential for the creation of feelings of belonging, significance and inclusion and a robust and clearly defined sense of self-identity.

Avoiding Helplessness

A felt sense of control is also required for avoiding helplessness. To stay in control of yourself and your life, you need to create a level of independence. You don't want to be subservient to others or trapped in a situation (like an unhappy marriage or an unfulfilling job). In short, you don't want other people or situations to have control over what you can do if you can avoid it. Thus generally avoiding helplessness, dependence and victimhood become central to the preservation of a healthy level of self-efficacy and self-determination.

Separateness and Relatedness

The duality of separateness and relatedness in social life (Layder 1997) expresses the tension between the need to establish and maintain your own personal space while also being involved in personal relationships. Being able to finesse this tension is always difficult because a move in one direction – say trying to get closer or more intimate with someone – always opposes the other side of the dilemma – in this case spending time on yourself and pursuing independent activities. Conversely, time spent away from your partner (depending on the circumstances and their emotional needs) might be perceived by them as a 'rejection' of their need for closeness and intimacy.

Emotional Intelligence

Being able constantly to readjust behaviour to mesh with others' needs, while ensuring that the ever-present tension between separateness (or aloneness) and relatedness (or involvement) doesn't get out of hand, is an important social skill sometimes referred to as 'emotional intelligence' (Goleman 1996). Without this, we would find it difficult to maintain relationships and keep them on an even keel. These and other skills concerned with identifying particular emotions and reading others' moods and feelings all contribute greatly to the extent to which we are able to feel 'in control' (or at least have some control) of ourselves, our relationships and our lives in general.

Reading others' emotions involves not only listening attentively to what they say, but also being able to interpret their feelings through non-verbal signals such as tone of voice, facial expression, gestures, posture and so on. The ability to read others' emotions accurately is an essential means of predicting what they are going to do or how they will react. It is a particularly important way in which people of lower social status or power are able to manipulate, resist or get round the demands of those who have more power.

But the same applies to less extreme disparities of 'interest' which commonly occur in routine encounters. For example, differences of opinion or clashing intentions are more smoothly managed if those involved can accurately read each other's non-verbal signals. Of course, the facility for reading emotions is a form of power and control in itself, because the ability to manage the emotions of others may have the effect of neutralizing whatever more 'conventional' power resources they possess such as age, expertise, authority and so on.

It's not just the management of others' emotions that is at stake here. Being able to manage your own feelings is also crucial because emotional self-control through the restraint of immediate impulses is important for success in life. Being able to delay gratification encourages self-motivated and effective behaviour. Holding back inappropriate expressions of feeling or controlling your temper are equally important. In this sense, self-control and the ability to control others are mutually intertwined.

Personal and Positional Appeals

Perhaps another way of describing some of the phenomena included under the label 'emotional intelligence' is better described as what Bernstein (1973; 1974) in his research on language and communication in families has referred to as personal control through the use of 'personal appeals' and which he contrasts with 'positional control and positional appeals'. In positional appeals, parents discipline their children with reference to their respective status positions. Thus parents trade on traditional authority over their children to back up any instructions or commands.

Positional control is reflected in expressions like 'Do as I say', or 'I'm your mother and I'm telling you that we are going to visit Granny'. Or 'you'd better go to bed or I'll tell your father'. In these cases, the child is given no degree of latitude as to how or whether they should comply, they are simply told to. The rule learned by the child is one that underlines the hierarchical character of formal status in society. Underlying the authority is the threat of sanctions such as being grounded, or the withdrawal of privileges like watching TV.

Personal appeals, by contrast, depend on enlisting the child's unique personality and personal 'take' on the world in order to encourage them to appreciate the underlying appropriateness of what their parent requires them to do. Thus the parent will explain why the child should do something (say, go and visit a grandparent) by laying out the reasons in the context of the child's personal relationship with the grandparent, their previous encounters, experience and attitudes. So, for example, it will be explained that the grandparent loves the child and that it will make them very happy if the child pays them a visit. The child is invited to connect emotionally and to identify with the possibility of visiting their grandparent and to understand what it means in terms of their own and others' feelings.

In principle the idea of personal control based on personal appeals is relevant to all kinds of informal interpersonal relationships. The essence of informality presumes a level of intimacy and access to personal information that could be manipulated to the advantage of anyone who cares to take advantage of it. But in fact, the exploitation of such intimate, personal knowledge is the basic currency of every kind of interpersonal transaction. Beyond the confines of adult–child relationships (or ones involving a formally defined disparity in power), we engage with others by trading on emotional information about each other, and 'glossing' it to our own advantage. For example, we can only elicit someone's trust through empathy and sympathy, which in turn requires emotional attunement and rapport. The only way we can successfully do this is by 'bargaining' with implicit, personal knowledge that we have of the other person. We rely on understanding how the personal qualities of those involved are entrained in fashioning some kind of interpersonal agreement about the issue at hand. In short, the use of personal appeals is the fundamental medium through which we exert most of (whatever) control we have over our personal lives and relationships.

Personal Significance

In one sense everyone needs to be thought of as significant, as an individual who stands out (at least minimally) against the mass of others who populate our social world. In fact, the very notion of identity depends (in some part) on the idea that we are distinguishable from others – that we have a separate existence, reputation and so on. The need to feel personally significant is inversely related to the robustness of self-identity. The more fragile the personal identity, the more a person will feel the need for a visible demonstration of personal significance.

Someone who feels they have failed to have an impact on their lives and experiences will eventually be in desperate need of self-validation. And this, at least in part, can only come from other people. Each of us must feel we have the unconditional right to be alive and to participate in social life as a 'nominal' equal. For most people, this urge for personal significance is fulfilled through the successful enactment of conventional roles such as 'parent', 'business person', 'friend', 'lover' and so on. In this sense personal significance is socially accounted for in an unproblematic manner.

However, for various reasons not all people are sufficiently satisfied by this kind of 'invisible' conformity. For them it is not enough to be thought of as blending in with the rest because this is the very root of their problem – an inability to feel significant. There are those who need to feel that they stand out from the rest of the crowd as a compensation for a lack of self-esteem or security. Here the craving for significance is an expression of a deeper craving for love, approval or acceptance denied in childhood and which persists in adult life as a thirst for emotional satisfaction. Such cravings for adoration, love and approval are common motives of those who pursue fame and celebrity. Being a pop star, a movie star, an entertainer of any sort, perhaps, expresses the need for more approval than is necessary for other people.

Negative Significance and Celebrity

It doesn't necessarily have to be a positive form of significance to allay intense emotional need and the anxiety that accompanies it. The craving for significance through celebrity can take a negative form, as in being a notorious criminal or a violent prisoner or 'public enemy number one'. Very often such individuals feel they have been overlooked by society in general or slighted or humiliated by others whose negative response is then perceived as a more general social rejection. The resentment generated by such experiences must then be 'avenged' or 'put right' by perpetrating extremely negative acts such as violence, rape or murder.

A definite element in the motivation of many serial murderers is the attainment of cult status or 'negative' celebrity as a means of making their mark on society and requiting their need for significance and importance. In this sense their crimes can be understood as attempts to impose some control over their lives and destinies. Often social isolation, marginalization, or lack of success creates an intense sense of insignificance and meaninglessness and a burning hunger to be thought of as a 'somebody', even if this is a 'somebody' whose social significance has been 'awarded' for all the wrong reasons.

A negative status which announces to the world 'I have been taken notice of as an irredeemably bad person' is deemed by them to be better than no status, no meaningful self-identity at all (Masters 1993, 1995). Such strategies provide a means of asserting the individual's identity and efficacy; it declares their 'right' to feel that they have some control over their lives and how others regard them as human beings. Thus the quest for personal significance is intimately tied to the question of the capacity for personal control and its implications for self-identity.

The Need for Personal Control

The following brings together the main themes covered in this chapter in terms of a series of propositions about the need for personal control.

1 Personal control is the attempt to cater for emotional needs and desires. It's about how you obtain what you need from yourself and others while maintaining good mental health.

2 Personal control is the means through which you make a difference to your world and have some say in the decisions and actions that shape your future life experiences – your destiny.

3 Self-identity is tied up with the issue of personal control. It is the basis on which a sense of efficacy, effectiveness and agency (or mastery) is confirmed and sustained in everyday life.

4 You can only influence the minds and hearts of others through personal control. It's the primary way in which you can make things happen and thus reduce the impact of things that seem to simply 'happen' to you.

5 The level, amount and quality of personal control influence the shape, intensity and direction of emotions and feelings.

6 Because of its close link with emotion, personal control is also impli-cated in the ability psychologically to energize ourselves and others (Collins 1983). Without this energy we would literally be unable to deal with the psychic complexity of other people, which in turn, would limit our capacity to interact with them.

7 Control allows us to deal with past, present and future as they impact on our everyday lives. Linking their influences together in a coherent manner is a feat of self-mastery in its own right. However, the ramifi-cations go deeper. Being able to organize them in a particular way is the key to being able to go forward into the future. Drawing on past experience and anticipating the future allows us to deal with the immediate demands of the present. These can range in intensity from how to respond to the sudden eruption of an argument, or simply knowing the next thing to say in a conversation.

8 Having some purchase on the different dimensions of time also helps us deal with other problems in social encounters. The first is the sheer unpredictability of other people. While we sometimes feel that we can predict the responses and even behaviour of certain individuals, there is also the uncertainty that they might confound us by radically upsetting our expectations. Of course, this is because all individuals are unique and (unless they are under some regime of extreme constraint) will always be capable of producing idiosyncratic responses. Furthermore, individuals vary in their volatility, eccentricity and unpredictability.

We can never be sure we will elicit our anticipated response (certainly not in its entirety), but being able to juggle with and manage the dimensions of past, present and future is essential in dealing with the unanticipated behaviour of others. Being able to readjust one's emotional and cognitive set as a flexible response to an environment of unpredictability draws on and tends to reproduce self-efficacy, effectiveness and a sense of agency.

9 Another problem adds to the unpredictability of individuals. This concerns the uncertainty of outcome of encounters and the consequent (subjective) uncertainty produced in those involved. The distinctive feature of this problem is related to the question of how we deal with an unknown future. The internal dynamics of any situated encounter are such that it always proceeds towards an indeterminate, open and unknown future. We can never be sure of the ultimate outcome of an encounter because the very process itself throws up new conditions, circumstances and responses that affect the outcome.

An example of this can be seen when a group of friends meet up to decide what they will do that evening. Individual desires and intentions have to be suppressed in order to accommodate the collective wishes of the group (which may, in fact be contrary to everyone's individual wishes). Each individual's moods, feelings and attitudes will disperse into, and intermix with, those of others in a complex form of 'contagion' which produces an emergent outcome, a collective expression different from individual intentions. Thus, entering every encounter is like starting out on a journey (albeit, usually brief) in which the destination is uncertain. It is this sense of uncertainty that initially prompts us to seek as much personal control as possible over the unfolding of the little drama that transpires when people come together.

Self and Society: Some Preliminary Conclusions

Although an understanding of the psychological aspects of personal control is important, the self cannot be understood outside the influence of social discourses (including ideology) or the influence of social system features like class, the distribution of material resources, gender and ethnicity, age, status, consumption patterns and the like. The social world both constrains and facilitates human behaviour. In this sense social forces exert a powerful formative influence over us as individuals even though our behaviour is never determined by it.

But we must also avoid the opposite mistake of assuming that there is no such thing as an individual with her or his own unique subjectivity or inner psyche. Sociologists and social psychologists often speak of individuals as if they had no reality outside the governing influence of social phenomena. They assume that the inner psyche or subjectivity has been thoroughly 'claimed' by social forces that exist all around it. Postmodernists and discourse analysts make this mistake as much as their structuralist forebears. Even those theorists who have accorded a greater level of freedom to the individual in their analyses (such as symbolic interactionists, ethnomethodologists, phenomenologists and structurationists) have fallen into the same trap. Their theoretical assumptions limit the subjective freedom of individuals to the domain of inter-subjective reality. Everything of subjective importance to the individual is somehow thought to be created by social (inter-subjective) reality.

Against this excessive social constructionism, it is essential that the subjective interior of the individual be accorded a role in its own right. It is here that personal control provides a bridge between *subjective reality*, as it is 'experienced' by the individual, and *social reality*, as it is shared by the many individuals who populate society. In this light the impulse and orientation to personal control mediate the relation between self and society. The arena of personal control is our most immediate point of engagement with social forces (such as discourses, systems and structures), and their influence. But an individual's contact with society is always mediated by everyday situated activities.

In a sense, personal control is already interpersonal in form because it can only manifest itself through interpersonal engagement. None the less, in the final instance, only the individual can finesse the tie between subjective attachment and social constraint. The impulse and orientation to personal control are thus the tie that binds. Once lured into the social arena, the individual becomes trapped and fixed within it. Thus individual behaviour is never entirely subjective in character. Since personal control is interposed between the self and the wider world, the bonds between agency and structure are both social and psychological in nature. But although social and psychological realities are intrinsically related, they possess their own characteristics and forms of influence. This must not be forgotten in the rush to merge them together in a way that cancels out their independence.

Summary

- Emotion is strongly influenced by control and vice versa, although neither is primary.
- Although saturated by emotion, the self is also an executive centre that organizes and shapes behaviour.
- The impulse to control one's environment develops in early infancy and continues to be of importance throughout adult life.
- Although often overlooked, benign control plays a central role in social life; social interaction is impossible without it.
- Benign control underpins many social skills and personal qualities, including emotional intelligence, personal appeals, a sense of efficacy and competence, self-confidence, self-esteem and personal significance. It also helps us to deal with uncertainty and unpredictability in encounters.
- The importance of individual subjectivity and the emotions must not be overlooked for a general understanding of social reality. Personal control finesses the tie between subjective desires and attachment to others with the constraints of the social environment.

3

Social Encounters

Preview

- The forms of anxiety and insecurity deriving from social encounters and how the individual deals with them.
- The individual's involvement with, and commitment to, social life as it is filtered through differing but closely related social domains (psychobiography, situated activity, social settings, contextual resources).
- The multi-faceted nature of power and its influence on interpersonal control.
- How individuals finesse the link between their inner subjective life and their everyday social relationships.
- Typical strategies of interpersonal control: altercasting; attractors and personal magnetism; seduction; complicity and mutual pacts; enrolment and people management; manipulation; coercion, violence and intimidation.

This chapter focuses on the nature of the relationship between the individual and society and how interpersonal control helps to finesse this link. It begins with a discussion of the forms of anxiety and insecurity that are constant features of social encounters and the manner in which interpersonal control is closely interconnected with them. The chapter then moves on to an examination of the individual society relationship in terms of the domains that form the substance of social reality and social life. The final parts of the chapter focus on the role of interpersonal control as a link between the individual with his or her social environment, including a description of typical strategies of control.

Personal Control and the Anxiety of Uncertainty

In the previous chapter it was noted that there are two sources of uncertainty associated with encounters. These are the (ultimate) unpredictability of individuals and the sheer fact of the 'unknowability' of the future as it continuously unfolds from the encounter itself. Although we have ideas, expectations or hopes that encounters will turn out in a certain manner (a successful meeting, a sad occasion, a thrilling experience), we cannot know for sure what the outcome will be because it really depends on what happens in the encounter – how it turns out. What was anticipated as a successful meeting may end up as a disaster because you misjudged one of the participant's intentions. What you thought would be a sad occasion might turn out to be more light-hearted because of an unexpectedly humorous incident. The thrilling experience you hoped for may actually transpire to be a disappointing waste of time. You can never know for sure in advance, it all depends on the way events unfold.

These sources of uncertainty create an interactional problem of sizeable proportions. How can, and how do we, as individuals, cope with this level of uncertainty and the anxieties it generates? This is where uncertainty and anxiety are related to the issue of personal control. The individual reduces levels of 'uncertainty anxiety' by being ready for any problems that may arise. In particular, a prior orientation to control allows the individual to prepare for any untoward events or happenings that may take them by surprise, causing them to lose composure and poise, not only subjectively, but also in the eyes of the other participants.

This involves 'going over' in your mind what you think might happen in a projected encounter. This can be seen most clearly in those situations where you most definitely need to be prepared for any number of unpredictable incidents. Going for a job interview typically involves mental preparation such as rehearsing your responses to possible questions that the interviewer might ask, or how you might deal with an unexpected line of questioning, or how you might respond to being asked something you know nothing about. For example, in the case of not knowing the answer to a question, should you try to bluff your way out or should you come clean and admit that you don't know? If the latter, should you just say you don't know, or should you say that you are a willing learner and that the job would increase your knowledge and experience in precisely this area?

It is best to decide in advance what sort of response you will make, otherwise you run the risk of looking silly or insincere, inflexible or insensitive – all impressions that would stand in the way of your being offered the job. In this sense a prior orientation to control through mental planning provides the individual with a means of 'locking onto' the evolving events and circumstances by tracing the arc of their potential control in circumstances as they arise. By entering encounters with the possibility of control in mind, we allow ourselves to off-load a weighty baggage of 'uncertainty anxiety' that might otherwise prevent us from entering into social relationships at all. The mental sketch of the anticipated control arc functions to convince us that we are, indeed, capable of going through with the encounter because we believe that effective control is possible.

But, of course, once entrained in the relative chaos of an encounter, all our best plans come to nought. Rather than a pre-established script, improvization and innovation become the order of the day as we confront the ever-changing currents of social interaction. For example, once at the job interview we might find that despite all our attempts to plan and thus control our behaviour at the interview, unforeseen events or circumstances work to thwart our intentions and expectations. The interviewer happens to be in bad mood and objects to your answers, or dislikes the way you are dressed, or it transpires that the competition from better-qualified candidates is very stiff. In this respect the prior 'plan' is only ever a rough guideline, creating a predisposition towards control. As soon as the action gets started, prior plans must be abandoned in favour of more detailed, adaptive responses that follow the ever-developing contours of the encounter.

A prior 'script' will simply serve as the starting point for extensive revisions, departures and elaborations required by the specific circumstances of the encounter. But mostly, the provisional sketch acts as a means and motivation – the propulsion – to get started (see also Turner 1962, for similar treatment of the interactional problems associated with role behaviour). The accretive and unfolding nature of encounters means that we can never fully or completely grasp it in a controlling sense. Its dynamic character ensures that it begins to slip through our fingers the very moment we try to grasp it. We can only ever achieve partial and fleeting control over the ongoing chaos of routine encounters.

Anxiety and Insecurity

Another dimension of uncertainty and anxiety has to do with the general nature and well-being of the self as it engages with the 'cut and thrust' of social interaction. The crucial vulnerability that the self is subjected to is that of ontological insecurity (Winnicot 1963; Laing 1969). To understand this, it is helpful to see it as an extreme version of what is ordinarily referred to as insecurity. In everyday conversation, when you describe someone (or you yourself) as 'feeling a bit insecure', you mean they are feeling sensitive, vulnerable and lacking in confidence. It may refer to a momentary phenomenon as when you suddenly feel intimidated by someone or it may apply to a more general and long-standing inability to deal with people in authority or feeling anxious about speaking in public.

In either case, the sufferer is usually partly aware of the problem and often tries to conceal it from others. In this sense, 'normal' insecurities are not disabling in that they do not bring our lives to a complete halt. We remain effective and our core sense of who we are is not damaged.

On the other hand, the ontological type is a more extreme, damaging and disabling form of insecurity. The sufferer feels completely drained of self-esteem, self-belief and self-confidence and is unable to make effective decisions and actions in daily life. Laing specifically describes ontological insecurity by comparing it with a state of security. The distinguishing features of insecurity are a feeling of unreality, an experience of 'deadness' rather than aliveness, a confusion around identity, a sense of estrangement from one's body and a general alienation from the self or a feeling of being inappropriate to life (Branden 1985).

Undoubtedly there is a sense in which early childhood experiences of intimacy with caretakers and the predictable routines of daily life (which create a sense of safety, comfort and familiarity) serve to underpin ontological security in adult life. However, contrary to Giddens's (1984) argument, there is no simple link between social routines and a person's experience of ontological security or insecurity. Nor is there an inoculation against insecurity received during early childhood experiences with a caretaker. Each of us has a unique form and amount of ontological security which may increase or decrease in response to different situations and junctures in our lives.

In fact, whether or not we feel secure depends on the unique complexion of our lives at particular points in time. Sure enough, in facing the routine problems that are the ordinary stuff of life, a feeling of security tends to dominate our general psyche and sense of self. However, the routine circumstances of life do not inevitably throw 'routine' problems in our paths. For example, establishing an intimate, romantic relationship with someone is not necessarily smooth and unproblematic. All sorts of confusions, misunderstandings and misreadings of the 'state of play' of such a relationship are normal accompaniments to the eventual establishment of trust and the level of emotional disclosure thereby made possible. For example, an eventually successful bond may actually be preceded by a great deal of uncertainty and anxiety as reflected in such self-searching questions as 'Are they ignoring me on purpose or are they trying to get my attention by making me a little jealous?', 'Is he or she trying to tell me they're not interested or are they giving me the green light?'

Also, the balance of power in an intimate relationship tends to alter over time and may cause one person to feel more insecure and vulnerable at times, making them 'clingy' and dependent while their partner feels the opposite. Furthermore, the extent of ontological security varies from situation to situation. You might feel confident about chatting to someone at a party but freeze with fear at the idea of making a public speech. Clearly some situations are fraught with potential anxieties (for example, formal rituals like marriage ceremonies, or receiving honours, or making an inaugural speech as a professor).

Other situations are numbingly bland in their anxiety-provoking implications (such as making a cup of coffee in the kitchen or purchasing a newspaper) and clearly do not generate uncertainties about self-worth and confidence, or a sense of unreality around self-identity. In this sense we cannot think of security or insecurity as a fixed quantum indifferent to the individual's constantly changing experience of the world. Neither must we assume that encounters inevitably produce emotional equanimity or coherence around self-identity. In fact, ontological security must be constantly accomplished during encounters. In this sense, rather than blending in with everyone else, to some degree we must be self-assertive and communicate to others that we are confident in our own views and capabilities.

In other respects ontological security must be 'fought for', otherwise it will be undermined by ruthless individuals who will seize on and exploit any points of weakness. For example, in a situation where a person is intimidated by other individuals because of the sheer force of their personality or expression, or because they are trying to impose their own opinions or agenda, the 'target' must fight for her or his own voice to be heard, and for their own sense of importance and self-belief to be taken into account. In this sense the establishment and maintenance of security are always 'in question' from the individual's point of view.

Conversely, the fragility of ontological security may be such that a thoughtless, insensitive comment, or the unforeseen eruption of an argument, may have the effect of undermining or severely denting self-belief. Depending on the psychological resilience of the individual, this may simply result in a minor and fleeting loss of composure. But if a person's mental life is already lacking in robustness, such incidents may initiate a critical questioning of one's intrinsic worth as a human being. In this respect ontological security is never finally 'won'; it is chronically contested during the interchanges that take place during an interpersonal encounter.

The establishment of ontological security can never be achieved in a mechanical fashion by the enactment of social routines and rituals. It always remains an 'unfinished' project which itself has no predictable outcome. Depending on the specific individual and the particular circumstances, a 'routine' encounter could turn out to be a very unpleasant and taxing experience, as in the example of meeting your long-term lover who, seemingly out-of-the-blue, announces that they want to end the relationship. Ontological security is an ongoing, emergent accomplishment and not a mechanical outcome of everyday routines. Thus it cannot be considered as a 'given', constant or steady-state accompaniment to social life (as Giddens (1984, 1991) argues). It is more accurate to think of it in terms of a partial, fleeting achievement, hewn from the 'chaos' of social interaction. Disappointments, fears, hatreds, anxieties and so on, always interpose themselves between the need for ontological security and its situational achievement (see Craib 1994).

Given its nature, ontological security is directly implicated in the same quest for control as a means to allay the anxiety caused by uncertainty. However, in this case the uncertainty and anxiety centre on self-identity rather than broader concerns about achieving a specific outcome from the encounter. The issue of control, then, is central to a diverse array of related aspects of anxiety and uncertainty. Unfortunately these aspects are rarely, if ever, differentiated from one another and hence their reciprocal influences remain largely unexamined.

The Domain of Psychobiography

All individuals carry 'normal' anxieties associated with personal authenticity, insecurity and the uncertainties of social interaction. Differences among individuals are marked by the extent to which they are able to deal with these anxieties on an ongoing basis. It is not the case that a happy, fulfilled and well-adjusted person doesn't have, or has never experienced such anxieties. Rather, such a person is one who has managed to deal with these anxieties so as to minimize their debilitating impact. The unhappy (perhaps mentally disturbed) person, on the other hand, is one who has been unable to deal with anxiety in this sense and has become overwhelmed by it.

The average, moderately well-adjusted individual manages to conduct his or her life free of extremely debilitating effects (such as social phobias, paranoia). Nevertheless such individuals are aware of the insidious manner in which little insecurities and social and personal anxieties sometimes 'intrude' into their personal and social life. Such responses may lend a certain complexion, character and individuality to a person's behaviour but they do not prevent them from leading a 'normal' life. Another way of putting this is that the uniqueness of each individual is an expression of how successful (or unsuccessful) he or she is in managing these existential anxieties. We may also conclude that this reflects their proficiency or effectiveness in the area of control (over self and others).

Coupled with the problems of avoiding helplessness, the need for significance and approval, the tensions between separateness and relatedness and so on, we can appreciate that individuals are strongly influenced (positively or negatively) by the impulse and readiness for control in everyday social interaction. But individuals also possesses a developmental history that has formed, and continues to help form them as unique self-identities. That is, the individual possesses a psychobiography that traces their lifelong personal development and individuation. Psychobi-ography records and maps an individual's engagement with a unique configuration of people and relationships, from childhood through to the latest point in their life career. But this is not simply an externally sign-posted map of life-events and emblems of personal development. Crucially it points to a psycho-emotional process of individuation, creating the person as a unique complex of emotional needs and behavioural responses.

Individuals, Relationships and Situated Activity

But how do these unique self-identities with their variable control capac-ities and tendencies engage with, or lock into, the wider social world? At first sight the primary point of contact with the social environment might seem to be social relationships – with family, friends, colleagues and acquaintances. This is true up to a point, but a personal relationship is not static or frozen in time, it is 'alive' and ever changing as the parti-cipants literally 'live out' their transactions with one another.

In this sense, relationships have no real meaning unless they are under-stood as intrinsic to the activities generated by the participants. Thus the relationship between a mother and her daughter is not simply the abstract expression of cultural expectations about how mothers and daughters have behaved towards each other in the past or how they should behave in the future. Rather a real relationship is about the actual way in which a mother behaves towards, and in concert with, her daughter. In short, a relationship is about the shared activities the participants engage in and how they act and interact with one another in specific situations.

Thus I use the term 'situated activity' to indicate the 'inner' coating of social connectedness for the individual. It is the first layer of social influ-ence as far as individual experience is concerned. Situated activity is a social domain (and a layer of reality) that differs from psychobiography and the other social domains I shall go on to describe. Psychobiography refers to specific individuals and their personal and social trajectories through time and space. It refers to the social and psychological influ-ences that have formed them as unique individuals with a coherent and relatively continuous self-identity. Thus, as a domain of social and psycho-logical reality, it differs considerably from situated activity.

Situated activity involves dynamic, person-to-person relationships between at least two individuals enclosed by the situational focus of their mutual involvement – for example, a party, chit-chat between friends, a formal business meeting or a transaction with a check-out clerk. In this sense situated activity is discontinuous and episodic. As Goffman (1967) points out, the elapsing of situated activity is marked by the arrivals and departures of those involved. Put slightly differently, situated activity begins (comes into existence) with the meeting of the individual participants and ceases to exist when they disassemble and go their separate ways.

The only 'form' in which the 'reality' of situated activity could be said to endure after the disassembly of the participants would be as a 'virtual' reality, as part of the memory traces of those who had participated. In that respect those same participants may bring with them to future (situated) encounters memories of the previous encounter; thus some of the 'unfinished' business may be carried over. Examples of this can be seen in the aftermath of an argument that continues to create tension in subsequent encounters, or conversely, when two people who are attracted to each other become emotionally closer with each encounter. Such continuities create punctuated sequences of situated activity that possess a thematic similarity.

In essence, situated activity is the pragmatic arena in which relationships are routinely lived and played out. They have an ongoing character but the actual scenes of activity are punctuated by the 'thereness' or presence/availability of the individual participants. Also, a consequence of this presence/availability is that in particular situations the individual participants are influenced by one another. Each person is both constrained and freed ('opened up') by the attitudes and behaviour of the others in their co-presence. Several writers have noted that it is in the area of face-to-face interaction that novel interpretations of the meaning of events are created through the resulting amalgam of different inputs of the participants.

In this sense, interactionists and phenomenologists like Mead (1967), Blumer (1969) and Garfinkel (1967) have argued that meaning is a situational accomplishment born out of the emergent and reciprocal responses of the interactants. For example, a man and woman are seen to exchange a brief kiss on the cheek as they pass in the corridor at work – what is the meaning of the kiss? As an observer, can we say that there is something objectively significant about such behaviour that furnishes us with its meaning? Further reflection may convince us that this is not the case because there are several possible (and potentially correct) interpretations.

It could indicate that the two involved are long-term partners who still make a point of demonstrating their affection. On the other hand, the perfunctory nature of the kiss may reflect the fact that the relationship is one based on 'friendship' rather than anything deeper. Yet again, the kiss may be vastly more significant if it hasn't happened before and is the prelude to a more intimate relationship. We can only understand the actual meaning of the kiss by acquiring inside knowledge of the participants, their intentions, their desires and the current status of their relationship. What the kiss means is what the kiss means to them, and how they respond to each other in performing the action itself. We can only know the meaning of events, therefore, by understanding how the behaviour of one person is interpreted by the other and vice-versa, in a chain of such responses.

But there are other behavioural phenomena that are unique to this domain. Goffman (1983) has claimed that what he calls the 'interaction order' encourages patterns of behaviour apart from the production of localized meaning. In this sense, the interaction order is a set of implicit rules about how people deal with one another in face-to-face interaction. It is concerned with how we take care of our own and others' self-identities through trust and respect and how we generally help each other out so that the encounter goes smoothly (Rawls 1987), as well as the idea that there is a pragmatic morality about fair dealings (Giddens 1987).

Thus we help each other out through trust, tact and the willingness to remedy or repair social gaffes and other 'mistakes' that are often made in transactions between people because we hope and expect they will do the same for us. While self-care, taken to an extreme, could result in the selfish manipulation of others, it is often balanced by the altruistic emphasis of the interaction order. This is so, even though this altruism is often 'conditional' upon the expectation that it will be applied to oneself in return.

Certainly, the influences of what Goffman terms the 'interaction order' are clearly felt in some guise in what I have termed 'situated activity'. However, as aspects of social reality, they remain very different – whereas Goffman speaks of them as if they were the same. But phenomena like rules and morality can never be construed simply as situational accomplishments. They have an integral connection to the wider reproduced, institutional elements of society (part of the outer wrap-around of social domains that encircle and contain individuals). Situated activity exists in relation to the arrivals and departures of relevant assemblies of people. It is episodic and evanescent and dependent entirely on the actualized transactions between real describable actors. By contrast, the interaction order is about the more generalized, abstract set of rules that may or may not be drawn upon by those involved in situated activity.

Take the rule of involvement, for instance. It suggests or implies that individuals should display an appropriate level of involvement in the presence of others. For example, if engaged in intimate behaviour such as kissing or sexual intercourse, one is not supposed to become involved in some tangential interest such as watching TV or listening to the radio. As culturally reproduced rules, 'involvement obligations' may set the widest parameters within which appropriate behaviour should fall, but the mere existence of the rule does not guarantee conformity with it, nor the stylistic form it may take. Rules (and the morality implicit in them) are inert symbolic resources that may be interpreted in many different ways, in accordance with the localized agreements and understandings. The behavioural manner and style that people adopt in actually 'doing' or 'performing' involvement ('cheeky' or 'pretend' involvement, as opposed to its more sincere and intense varieties) is what is germane to situated activity, not the existence of the rule itself.

Social Settings and Individual Behaviour

Psychobiography and 'situated activity' are quite distinct although closely interrelated domains of social reality. Situated activity (along with social relationships) is the proximate (most immediate) wrap-around layer of social reality from the point of view of individual experience. Continuing with the imagery of 'layers' or 'coatings', the next outer layering is occupied by what I term 'social settings'. All situated activities exist in a wider social environment of position-practices. Thus social settings form the immediate 'environment' of situated activity. Social organizations such as factories, hospitals, schools, military barracks, universities and so on are examples of the most sharply defined settings. Informal relationships like family and friendship networks are examples of more dispersed, loosely organized, less patterned and defined settings.

Importantly, settings are contiguous with situated activity and are thus the individual's closest point of contact with society or the 'social system'. As such they are localized clusters of social constraints and enablements. Although many of the more informal settings of everyday life are characterized by loosely defined position-practices, this simply means a wider latitude for individual interpretations and hence, for uniquely customized behaviour. For example, settings of friendship or informal, caring behaviour are classic examples of voluntary emotional commitments and 'obligations'. They contrast sharply with those found, say, in work organizations, which rely on surveillance and the enforcement of company rules and procedures.

Although social settings are the immediate environment of situated activity, they also represent a distinctly formed domain of social reality. Unlike situated activity, they are formed out of reproduced or institutionalized, social relationships. They are not free-forming assemblies and disassemblies of people operating within specific situations. They are the socially organized conditions (reproduced relations) under which different kinds of situated activity take place. Such settings are often associated with physically discrete or segmented locations, such as a factory, an office, a home, a street; but the real distinguishing characteristic is their socially organized and reproduced nature as a set of position-practices.

The Outer Layer: Contextual Resources

If the individual is the heart of successively enveloping layers of social reality, we now come to the outermost layer (and social domain) – that of contextual resources. This represents a person's most general social influences and has several elements. First are society-wide inequalities of material and social capital. Belonging to groups defined in terms of these patterns of inequalities such as class, gender, ethnicity, age, illness and so on, has significant and often profound effects on a person's intellectual and social capabilities as well as her or his social destiny.

But contextual resources also refer to the vast array of 'stored' knowledge (cultural, ideological and institutional) accumulated over the generations. These provide an even more inclusive backdrop to the individual's existence. This stored knowledge includes the printed media, such as books, journals, magazines, newspapers, advertisements, documents of all kinds, as well as visual media like television, films, video, computers and so on. Typically there are links between these different kinds of contextual resources. An individual's social destiny, personality and personal capacities may be influenced by the effects of class or ethnic belonging combined with the kind of discursive material to which they are exposed, both socially and educationally. But not all discursive materials are tightly linked to distributive and membership groups in this manner. They are often more loosely coupled and, as a consequence, influence behaviour rather more diffusely.

All in all, contextual resources influence individual behaviour by providing general cultural parameters in the form of expectations, custom, tradition, mores, habits, rules, and so on. But they do so by linking in with settings and situated activities that mediate and mutually condition their influence. Conversely, individuals continually reproduce contextual resources by using them in their everyday activities.

Social Domains and Individual Behaviour

While the private subjectivity of the individual is never fully constructed through social influence, at the same time, individuals are never apart from the social arena. As Figure 3.1 makes clear, the individual social agent is enmeshed in ever more general and inclusive domains. As a consequence, causal influences run in all directions simultaneously, from inner to outer layers and back again. Nevertheless, situated activity is the main gateway between individual agency and the (social) systemic domains of settings and contextual resources. This highlights the pivotal role played by situated activity in understanding interpersonal relations. In the practical reality of everyday life, social domains are bound together

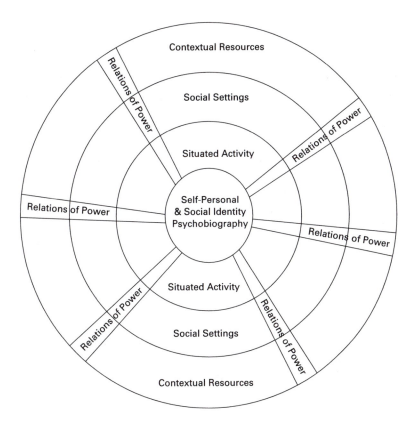

Figure 3.1   Social Domains & Relations of Power

via social relationships that contain and conduct their influence. The role of power and control is also crucial here. Since social relationships are intrinsically relations of power, they are never neutral or 'innocent' in their operations or effects.

Interpersonal Power and Control

Many analyses of power assume that it exists in one form only, even though analysts differ as to what that form is. This stance merely hampers an understanding of power as existing in (different) forms and deriving from different domains of social reality. Power in situated activity is distinctive in that it is an emergent amalgam of powers originating in other domains. It is the point of confluence of individual and structural (or systemic) forms of power.

Interpersonal control then, is the process by which people draw upon the variety of power resources originating from different social domains.

As an individual responds to others, he or she draws on personal powers such as charisma, physical or psychological attractiveness, and expertise in the manipulation of others. But at the same time, whatever status or position they hold in the relevant setting (for instance, formal authority at work or parental status in a family) are power resources that can be drawn into activity.

The same holds for those elements of discourse, class, gender, ethnicity and other contextual features that are of direct relevance to the situation. These are either filtered through the immediate social setting or make themselves felt in activity because of their more general social relevance (such as social conventions like manners, etiquette, values or ideology). All such power influences and resources enter the mix of situated activity as and when drawn on by participants.

Situated activity is, therefore, a 'gathering point' of power resources that may be drawn on by those involved to underpin their interactional exchanges. But individuals make their powers 'stick' effectively by drawing upon only those powers that are relevant to the situation at hand – such as skills in persuasion, rhetoric, personal magnetism, charisma, material possessions, social status, cultural capital, formal positions, roles or authority. Not all potential resources will be relevant at any one point in time, but they are available should the need arise.

This is particularly so where individuals' priorities change as the situation unfolds, requiring recourse to other power resources. This leads to a repositioning of the individual in the encounter and a shift of emphasis in their power plays and control strategies. Consider, for example, a person who habitually relies on personal magnetism or physical attraction in order to assert control and get what they want. If they find themselves in a situation in which these 'charms' are no longer effective (for example, being stopped and questioned by the police, or being refused entry to a club or bar), they will need to employ other forms of power and influence – say, their formal work status or family connections – to adjust to their 'repositioning'. Of course, each individual will have their own 'unique' power resources – their special qualities and skills. This makes for a fine-grained intermeshing of influences. The overall configuration of power and control and the emotional tenor of encounters will thus be constantly reshaped according to emergent circumstances and the unique contributions of the individuals involved. The exact mix of power influences at any one time will, therefore, be a unique amalgam deriving from different social domains.

This multi-dimensional model of power and control differs radically from those that assume that it has one (ontological) form. This view is exemplified by those who view power as exclusively linked to discursive practices (Foucault, social constructionism and discourse analysis), or as a form of domination and oppression (Marx, Habermas (1984, 1987), or as the action of specific actors over others (individual or collective) to achieve their ends, and so on (Weber (1964), Giddens (1984), symbolic interactionism). The multi-dimensional model recognizes power as emanating from different ontological features (domains) of society.

The phenomenon of interpersonal control is dynamic and ontologically mixed. The acting individual is the 'eye of the storm', the centre of a maelstrom of diverse powers and their effects. The person, therefore, is embroiled in a range of power effects (behavioural consequences) that are both differentially available to specific actors, and differentially employed by them as they move through the unfolding experience of specific encounters.

Strategies of Control: Altercasting

Sociologists working within the symbolic interactionist tradition have focused on issues associated with interpersonal control. For instance, Weinstein has noted that in order to be 'interpersonally competent', it is pivotal that individuals possess skills 'at establishing and maintaining desired identities both for oneself and for others' (1963: 757). Weinstein and Deutschberger (1963) suggest that the concept of 'altercasting' usefully captures the manner in which the identity-related aspects of interpersonal control are achieved.

Altercasting involves 'casting' the other into an interactional role that is supportive of one's own identity in an impending performance. In a sense people co-opt others' behaviour in order to achieve their own purposes. As the authors put it, altercasting is 'projecting an identity to be assumed by others with whom one is in interaction which is congruent with one's own goals'. They see this as 'a basic technique of interpersonal control' (Weinstein and Deutschberger 1963: 454). More recently, Malone (1997) has demonstrated the usefulness of the concept of altercasting in the analysis of conversations. As Malone points out, 'in order to be interactionally successful, we must be able to get others to act in concert with our own desires' (1997: 110).

Malone suggests that in conversations, altercasting is an important means of avoiding conflict or disagreement, especially when you anticipate that what you have to say may be resisted or contested by someone else. In such cases altercasting can be achieved through three complementary but subtle manoeuvres. The first involves trying to establish a common bond and identity with the other person by suggesting an apparent sharing of knowledge about a particular subject or conversational topic. The use of phrases like 'you and I both know' or, 'we are very much alike in this respect', allow an apparent sharing of goals and purposes to be subtly imported into the discussion.

Second, altercasting is achieved by suggesting agreement or apparent agreement. By seeming to agree with someone by saying 'well we are very much in agreement as far as that is concerned' or 'of course you are right on this', you enlist them as a supporter of your own views and the identity you are currently projecting. Third, altercasting is made possible by using what Malone calls 'mitigation' in conversational talk, involving the use of such things as politeness markers, hesitation, rephrasing or the addition of unnecessary words and phrases. This helps to soften requests and so reduces the potential for face-threatening incidents.

Without doubt, altercasting is an important and useful tool for the analysis of strategies and techniques of interpersonal control. However, as currently formulated, it underplays the role of emotion in desire. It stresses how we manage to get others 'in line' with our own goals by relying heavily on our cognitive capacities and their rational deployment. However, it is a mistake to isolate cognition and perception (indeed, any mental processes) from emotion and feeling. Interactional exchanges have an intrinsically emotional nature. Thus it is necessary to add to the notion of altercasting several other concepts that more directly convey the emotional tenor of interactional exchanges.

Attractors and Personal Magnetism

Individuals attempt to 'attract' or 'magnetize' the kind of attention they require to meet their psychological and emotional needs. In this sense the bodily self and personality are often regarded as 'commodities' that have an exchange value in the interpersonal marketplace. Thus, some attractive personal quality such as physical beauty, personality, demeanour, or an interpersonal skill such as being able to make others feel at ease, being a good conversationalist or being exciting company, is exchanged for the attention and positive regard of others.

Although many such attractors may be regarded as 'given', for example, physical beauty, or being good at chit-chat, they are often not enough in themselves to sustain their magnetic appeal beyond an initial period. People therefore tend to 'work at' developing and honing what they regard as their 'best' qualities, attributes or skills in order that they can 'lead with their strengths' in the interpersonal arena. In this sense magnetism and attraction are 'democratically' distributed in so far as everyone is capable of making 'the best' of themselves.

However, some unique personal qualities are more rare and more compelling than others. Max Weber (1964) captured this idea with his concept of 'charismatic leadership' which he discussed in the context of a more general discussion of types of authority. Thus unique charismatic qualities can elevate particular individuals into 'leaders' or 'gurus' able to attract a group of followers who may pledge their allegiance and loyalty to them. As the examples of Jesus Christ and Adolf Hitler clearly show, such leadership qualities can be used in the service of good or evil depending on the person and the social circumstances.

But even in our everyday interpersonal dealings we attempt, in much smaller ways, to attract others by presenting ourselves to them in a manner that emphasizes our most prized interpersonal assets or attributes. In this sense individuals 'advertise' their best qualities to others in the hope of creating a magnetic forcefield. As with the larger example of charisma, the attempt to exploit our most compelling qualities to feed our psychoemotional needs can be associated with either benign or malign purposes.

Seduction

The word 'seduction' is usually associated with strategies or games as preludes to sexual intimacy. However, seduction has a broader meaning that centres on the ability to entice, beguile or lure. Seduction may be employed in conjunction with other strategies, although attraction or magnetism largely depend upon the possession of a commodity (an attractor) that can be offered in an emotional exchange. But to make seduction work on its own terms requires more in the way of deliberate effort and persuasion. Seduction relies on the use of gentle enticements and lures because the employment of heavy-handed techniques or 'obvious' manipulation will be 'seen-through' and will thus prove counterproductive.

However, seduction is not necessarily associated with benign purposes or intentions. In fact, techniques of seduction are particularly effective when used in conjunction with domination, exploitation and violence. In this respect the aura surrounding seduction tends to pacify the target or victim and makes the manipulation easier to achieve. The objective of the perpetrator is to deceive the target into thinking that the situation is benign and that they can therefore let down their guard. Horley (2000) notes that men who abuse women make extensive use of 'charm' before and after bouts of violence in order to unsettle their victims and make their own behaviour as unpredictable as possible. While such outward charm creates an illusion of benign seduction, it is part of a wider pattern of deception and exploitation and thus cannot be considered as real seduction.

Although this kind of 'illusory' seduction is an important prelude to some instances of domination or violence, seduction proper is typically associated with benign control and milder, gentler forms of manipulation. The sincerity of the seducer is thus an important ingredient of the process of seduction itself. This is essential because seduction often works through the exchange of 'emotional gifts' used as lures to tempt the 'target' into compliance. The use of charm as a 'persuader' will only work if the anticipated emotional pay-off really does happen. Saying that you will love someone even more than you already do, if they go along with your ideas, will fall on stony ground if you have a reputation for false promises.

Likewise seduction depends on intimate emotional knowledge of the other. Being able to read the emotions and non-verbal signals given off by the intended target is essential to successful seduction. The person who is the target of your seductive ploys will not open up or fall for enticements or lures unless you press the appropriate emotional buttons. In addition to knowing a person's sensitivities and vulnerabilities, seduction also requires particular stylistic techniques in order to be successful. The way you ask for something, your tone of voice, your facial expression, the exact choice of words, may all be crucial to the eventual outcome. Over-all the seducer's ability to project a self-identity that is sincere, genuine and trustworthy is pivotal.

The use of teasing, flattery or gentle sarcasm (Vaitkus 1991) may also increase the seducer's appeal to the seducee. Of course, it is essential to employ them judiciously because unless the right note is struck, they can all too easily be misinterpreted and hence work against the goal of per-suasion. In this sense seduction is only properly effective if the seducee feels on equal terms with the seducer. In reality this means that the seducee must be genuinely part of the decision-making process. They will automatically resist if they feel pressurized.

Complicity and Mutual Pacts

More often than not, seduction remains unacknowledged and becomes a tacit part of a relationship – even though each person may be more or less 'privately aware' of what is happening 'beneath the surface'. By contrast, creating mutual pacts (and abiding by them) involves more open, con-sciously elaborated 'agreements' about shared responsibilities, under-standings and expectations. Also there is open recognition of the rewards that would accrue from keeping to 'the rules'.

Although many such pacts will be emotional in nature, this will be upfront and in the service of mutual support. But this in itself may have either positive or negative implications. For example, a husband and wife (or same-sex partners) may agree to divide responsibilities on matters of emotion in order to prop up mutual personal failings. Thus one partner may tolerate the other's dislike of discussing matters of intimacy or parti-cipating in sexual activity, while in return they are not pressurized about visiting relatives or socializing generally.

Another such a 'negative' pact would be where one partner takes main responsibility for doing emotion work (sorting out feelings and working around sensitivities) while the other concentrates on purely practical matters (managing finances, arranging building work, keeping the car in good order and so on). This resembles the stereotype of a gender division of labour, where it is claimed that women are more emotionally attuned and men more at home with practical matters. In reality, of course, such 'roles' are often reversed, but the example highlights the widespread existence of negative pacts. But positively charged pacts also abound. Agreements about who does what and when in terms of housework, child minding, leisure pursuits and socializing are sometimes enforced by the practicalities of modern life. As long as it is, indeed, an agreed pact and not the result of some inertial slide into habitual routine, then each person will gain some emotional satisfaction from the arrangement.

Despite the emotional implications of pacts, compared with seduction they are rather 'formal' in nature. The agreement is of the kind, 'if I do this for you, then you'll do that for me' and as such is governed by explicit rules, which if breached will result in tension or open conflict. Unlike seduction, the bargain that is struck is explicit and well defined rather like a pre-nuptial agreement, although not necessarily codified or in written form. Seduction, by contrast, rests on a tacit and rather fuzzily defined emotional understanding and the participants are either compliantly drawn along by the process itself, or they remain stubbornly resistant to its temptations.

Enrolment and People Management

Much interpersonal control relies on the employment of enrolment and people management skills. Such skills allow an individual to 'handle' others and bring them 'on side' by taking their point of view, their experience and their personality into account, and shaping their behaviour to fit in with their own interests, plans and goals. Such skills are particularly important in work settings that provide community services (such as nursing, teaching, social and probation work, reception work), in which there is constant person-to-person interaction.

Knowing how to deal with irate, angry or otherwise fractious clients or customers is of pivotal importance in allowing the 'service interaction' to proceed on a relatively smooth basis. Hochschild's (1984) study of airline flight attendants in the USA describes how 'people management' skills are utilized by employing companies to make the attendant's work easier. Attendants are trained to use their emotional responses (such as courtesy and projecting a happy, smiling demeanour) to deal with troublesome customers and create an atmosphere of calm and safety as well as a favourable image of the airline company.

But in everyday interaction, enrolment and management skills are of immense importance for navigating around and through personal relationships. By providing us with the tools to finesse our relationships with others, they allow our own psychological and emotional needs to be catered for as we simultaneously 'manage' others' sensitivities and needs. Empathy is a crucial element here and involves putting yourself into others' shoes to see the situation from their point of view.

Associated skills include 'listening' and being able to read non-verbal signals and other emotional expressions. Good listening primarily entails leaving 'space' for others to speak and suppressing one's own tendency to talk, and hence dominate conversations. But it also requires the sensitive 'probing' (asking questions) of others when they are confused or reluctant to express their feelings. Being able to identify one's own and others' emotions and to respond appropriately to them, is associated with what Goleman (1996) refers to as 'emotional intelligence'.

These interpersonal skills also involve the ability to pick up what Tannen (1987, 1992) terms 'meta-messages' in conversation, talk, and non-verbal signals such as facial expression, tone of voice, gestures and so on. Meta-messages are not explicitly stated but comment on the current 'quality' of relationships (the extent to which those involved are happy with each other). Unless both partners can read the messages that are being conveyed (beyond the words used) in conversations, then an important means of mutual control will be lost and the quality of the relationship will suffer.

Manipulation

Manipulation can occur in soft or hard guises. When combined with the strategies discussed above, elements of self-serving manipulation represent the softer or gentler guises. Thus seduction, enrolment or people management skills coupled with a greater emphasis on self-gain provide good examples of this softer version of manipulation. Healthy control in everyday life is based on mixed motives. In trying to get what we want, we tend to vacillate between selfishness and altruism.

Harder forms of manipulation cross the boundary into unambiguous selfishness on a more or less permanent basis. Regardless of its original causes, extreme self-centredness (such as insecurity, or some other 'inner' failing), the characteristic that distinguishes this pathological form of manipulation from its healthier counterpart, is the total displacement of empathy. In this respect the manipulator attempts to mould and channel the desires of the 'target' so that they are totally consonant with their own. In the process the manipulation becomes exploitative rather than merely selfish.

Manifestations of this, such as emotional blackmail, psychological manipulation and emotional terrorism, are prevalent in benign and emotionally conducive settings such as the family. There is a pathologically competitive dimension to these control strategies in which the 'controller's' interests, desires and needs are pitched against those of the victim and 'must' win out at all costs. It is as if the aim of life were to always get the better of someone else and to 'steal' their energy, happiness, independence and security. In what Redfield and Arienne (1995) call 'control dramas', such forms of manipulation are played out in ruthless contests of deception, the laying of guilt and emotional exploitation. Often such dramas are enacted entirely in psychological terms with threats of the withdrawal of love, approval, permission and so on thrown in as supportive ammunition. The power of psychological defeat in such contests should not be underestimated. Wars of mental attrition are also typical.

Coercion, Violence and Intimidation

The final step on the ladder of exploitative and manipulative control involves the more or less complete abandonment of talk and communication as means of obtaining compliance. Of course, talking and otherwise communicating with the 'target' (or, more appositely, the 'victim') are not entirely outlawed as such, but the foundation of the control technique fundamentally shifts over to coercion. Thus talk and communication become primarily concerned with issuing instructions or 'orders' to the victim rather than real mutual exchange. Genuine communication becomes effectively closed to the victim and thus degenerates into a one-way flow.

Although the actual use of violence and physical force may or may not play a part in the proceedings (depending on the circumstances and the objectives of the perpetrator), the implied threat is always in the background and could act as a back-up if resistance were encountered. In many cases, such as robbery, hold-ups, rape, kidnapping and hijacking, threats and intimidation become the immediate and most important currency of control. It is usually only if victims refuse to be as submissive and malleable as the controller wishes that the actual use of force and violence will come into play.

In other anti-social and criminal activities, violence is used as a deliberate adjunct. For example, the use of violence as a 'punishment' (as in a gangland beating, or women abuse) or when the physical aggression is the whole point of the activity such as in street brawls or gang fights. When it becomes an integral part of the act, violence is inevitable, as in certain forms of sado-masochism, or in mass or serial murder.

These instruments of control represent extremes of selfishness or self-orientation whereby the interests, desires and needs of the victims are extinguished entirely. Control is simply appropriated; no consent is sought and no negotiations are entered into. The controller's purposes and objectives are paramount. Thus in many instances of gratuitous violence, rape or murder, the perpetrator (they are mainly men) experiences a desire to exert total control over his victims, and actively attempts to do this (even though the actual accomplishment of 'total' control is illusory). In many cases the human status of the victims is also disregarded. Perpetrators lack the ability to feel empathy for their human victims.

Summary

- Anxiety generated by uncertainty in encounters, and anxiety deriving from threats to ontological security, are closely connected with issues of emotion, personal identity and interpersonal control.
- From the point of view of the individual, his or her experience is filtered through the influence of different domains of social reality; psychobiography, situated activity, social settings, contextual resources. Interpersonal control must be understood in relation to these interconnected domains.
- Power is multi-faceted. Situated activity is the meeting point for the influence of powers deriving from different social domains. Interpersonal control is the active expression of these interconnected sources of power.
- An important way in which we, as individuals, finesse the link between our subjectivity and the social environment is by engaging in control strategies.
- The importance of benign control in everyday life has been underestimated and under-examined. There are many shades of benign control and strategies associated with it. They include: altercasting, attractors and personal magnetism, seduction, complicity and mutual pacts, enrolment and people management.
- At the other end of the spectrum, interpersonal control is more manipulative. In its extreme form it includes coercion, violence and intimidation.

4

Types and Dimensions

Preview

- The chapter presents an overview of types of interpersonal control.
- At one end of the spectrum are the healthy, benign forms of control commonly found in everyday life.
- At the other end are the pathological types, the most extreme of which involve domination and exploitation.

Having so far considered interpersonal control in a wider context of theoretical issues, it is now time to examine its more practical aspects. What types of control are there? What are the properties and dimensions of control? What strategies of control are employed by individuals in their situated activities? In the first instance we may understand types of control on a continuum ranging between 'benign control' at one end to exploitative control or domination at the other.

From Benign to Exploitative Control

Acknowledging the existence of benign control importantly corrects the popular assumption that control per se should be condemned as wrong or evil and must be eradicated. As we have seen, control is an intrinsic feature of human agency and ties self-identity to wider social system elements. Control is also, therefore, an intrinsic feature of social life in general. However, the main modes in which this control is exercised need to be distinguished. The concept of benign control is pertinent to a large sweep of social behaviour that has more than self-interest as its main point of reference.

Benign control is the most basic means of exerting influence over others, although this seems little appreciated in the popular imagination as well as in the more formal analytic literature on power and control. The common thread in all control is that it is aimed at securing the compliance of the target. However, the mode of its accomplishment and the exact nature of the intended outcome can vary considerably. This is clearly illustrated if we consider benign control in relation to its polar opposite, domination.

Benignity in control is reflected in its attempt to take the interests of others at least partially into account. By contrast, in domination the interests of the more powerful person are overriding. Also, benign control is inherently partial and open-ended. Since the use of benign control is intended to influence or persuade, rather than force another to comply, it is crucial that the target be allowed some voice in proceedings. Thus communication in benign control is based on a two-way flow of information between those concerned. It is also 'mutual' in so far as 'controlling plays' are met with counter 'plays'. A cycle of moves and counter moves which trigger further responses and counter responses is set in train and creates a cumulative little history of its own. However, the control remains benign only as long as a broadly equal reciprocity is maintained, where each party has an opportunity to 'have their say' and 'get their way'.

The aim of domination is total control of the other (or others), in which their autonomy is completely suppressed or negated. It is associated with an array of coercive measures including deception, slavery, hostage taking, kidnapping, ransom, torture and violence – sometimes including murder. The victim must comply irrespective of their powers of resistance and capacities to do otherwise. Unfortunately, under the influence of Weber's (1964) writings, domination has been taken as a general model for power.

But power is about control and influence in relation to the intended outcome of compliance and this is clearly a central feature of benign control. It differs from domination in terms of its mutual and reciprocal nature, its open channels of communication and its attempt to enrol the subjectivities of those who are its targets. These differences ensure that benign control does not fit the conventional, Weberian model of power relations. But to deny that benign control is a form of power would be to deny the variegated spectrum of control in everyday life. It would also fail to recognize an ontological continuity in forms of power.

Types of Interpersonal Control

The principal types of control are represented in Figure 4.1, which traces the movement from mutual benign control to full exploitative domination.

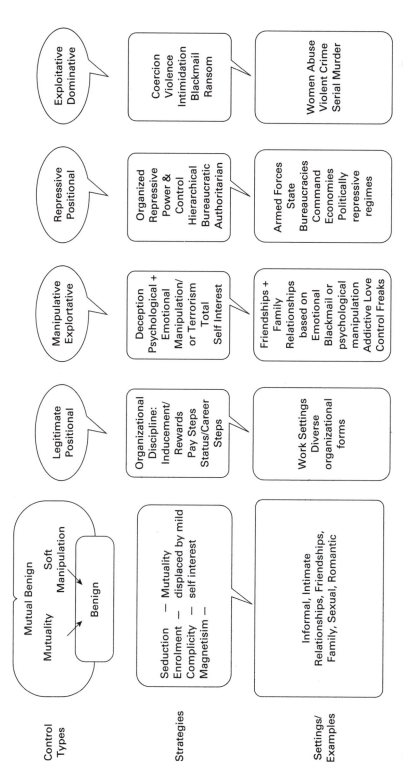

Figure 4.1 Types Strategies and Examples of Interpersonal Control

This also follows the transition from 'normal' or 'healthy' control to the pathological types of varying intensities. There is a continuity between what are regarded as legitimate, socially acceptable types of control and those involving more anti-social and 'unhealthy' aspects. This continuity reflects the common thread in all forms of control – the ability to get others to do what we wish and to support us in our aims and purposes.

Mutual benign control must be considered alongside the *benign-manipulative* type because they often occur in conjunction with each other. The completely pure forms of these are less common than the mixed types. Mutual benign control, in which each person gains something of value or broadly 'equivalent' satisfaction from an encounter or a relationship, is usually only achieved for relatively short periods of time and only with others who are equally committed to maintaining such a balance.

That mixed types are more prevalent than pure ones is because of the imperfect character of human beings. There are, perhaps, some individuals who achieve an almost saintly selflessness but this is rare because of the difficulty of maintaining such a spiritual state of mind on anything more than a transitory basis. Most of us are somewhat less than saintly in our everyday dealings with others partly because of the persistent need to be self-preservative. We cannot afford to be too open, or vulnerable to potential exploitation by others, lest our own sense of confidence and esteem desert us as a consequence.

Often, despite our best intentions, in encounters or established relationships we are inclined to cement altruism with a spot of 'innocent' manipulation in which we tend to 'camouflage' the interests of others in what we consider to be their long-term 'best interests'. In so doing we 'push' our own views and interests at the expense of others. Also we regularly undergo transformations in self-identity (and hence in mood and disposition) that involve shifts of emphasis in the strategies of control we routinely employ. In this respect, 'average' everyday behaviour is a fairly balanced oscillation between these types. The self-protective and self-interested tendency never completely outstrips the altruistic, empathetic impulse, while the manipulative tendency never results in totally self-serving manipulation. This reflects the mixed-motive nature of human behaviour as noted by Schelling and Goffman.

The typical settings of *legitimate positional authority* differ from those associated with the types of control already discussed. These settings are more formal and crystallized and less intimate or personalized. There is a greater importance attached to formally defined position-practices in hierarchical organizations like government bureaucracies or the armed forces. Work environments, though, exhibit a diversity of arrangements, mechanisms and modes of control (hierarchical, flat, external, internal, central, dispersed, visible, invisible). However, a positional and authoritative underpinning remains crucial.

There is also a shift in another dimension. Positional authority rests more squarely on instrumental foundations than those in informal settings. A person subject to such authority is regarded more as an 'object' to be shaped and guided by the organization than a unique, emotional being. Some such work organizations are rather more caring and human towards their employees, but because of their essentially disciplinary character, tolerance for unique emotional factors is limited. They cannot be allowed to compromise wider and more encompassing objectives. Thus the 'effectiveness' of procedures and the smooth running of the organization (rather than the well-being of the employees) is paramount, whether this be measured in terms of continuing financial viability (as in many work organizations) or in 'league tables' of performance typical of state-controlled service occupations like hospitals, universities and schools. As a consequence, there is a greater prevalence of instrumental attitudes towards employees.

Of course, this is a matter of degree and emphasis. Emotionality and empathy can never be wholly shunted out of relationships in the work arena any more than elements of instrumentality can be totally removed from more intimate relationships (contra Habermas's 1984, 1987 views). Informal relationships between work mates or colleagues as well as locally defined work practices cannot be entirely excluded from work organizations. In any case, because of the emotionally saturated (but not necessarily irrational) nature of human behaviour, it always contains some personalized elements.

Pathological Types: Over-control

In pathological control, all hints of altruism and empathy are pushed far into the background. The controller's interests are pre-eminent and the sole objective is to gain the compliance of those subjected to their demands. The operation of this kind of control requires rather more behind-the-scenes manoeuvring on behalf of the controller. This is clearly so in the case of *manipulative-exploitative control*, in which the manipulation becomes harder and more serious. Cases of emotional blackmail and other kinds of psychological pressure (such as control freakery) in families in particular (but also in many other settings and relationships) clearly reflect this hardening of manipulation. The term 'control freak' tends to be misleadingly over-used in modern parlance but generally refers to the behaviour of those who 'keep their cards close to their chest' and retain control over everything that concerns them.

Manipulation of this sort eats into intimacy in a more insidious form in co-dependence or addictive love. In these both partners are locked into mutual manipulative control in the hope that this will guarantee the continuance of the relationship. I deal with this in more detail in the next chapter but it is clear that such symbiotic relationships are products of the psychological insecurity of those involved.

Repressive-authoritarian control is the direct counterpart of positional control in the context of legitimate authority. A common feature is the importance of defined position-practices to their overall operation. They also share its disciplinary character and a reliance on modes of surveillance to uphold the practices that constitute their organizational settings. The principal distinguishing feature of this kind of control is the socio-political context in which it is embedded.

Repressive or dictatorial political regimes tend to rely on ideological manipulation of the mass of the population, in which communication between controllers and controlled is exclusively 'closed' or one-way. The overwhelming objective is the implementation of orders or directives and not (democratically) participative decision-making. This strict hierarchical control is generally situated in bureaucratic and militaristic forms of organization. Clarity and definition of position-practices ensure the smooth functioning of the hierarchy and accentuate the accountability and efficiency of surveillance mechanisms.

Finally, *dominative-exploitative control* is the epitome of repressive control in that it depends on maximum restraint of the victim and the perpetrator's ability to wield total control. The emphasis is on coercion rather than persuasion, although 'persuasion' may be used as a supportive adjunct to coercion. Violence, intimidation and torture are the stock-in-trade of the dominative-exploitative type. However, the more compliant the victim is, the easier becomes the perpetrator's task. Thus the deliberately deceptive use of 'softer', seemingly more benign control has the effect of enlisting the 'trust' of the victim. Also the unpredictable switching between hard and soft techniques can have a damaging effect on the resilience of the victim.

Dominative exploitation can take a variety of forms. Domestic violence or women abuse exhibits many of the features mentioned above, including the selective use of 'softer' techniques of persuasion. The male perpetrators often use it as a smoke-screen that prevents outsiders from realizing that abuse is really occurring inside the relationship. However, the ultimate expression of this type of control is in serial murder in so far as absolute control over the life or death of another becomes an end in itself.

This brief overview of types of interpersonal control serves as an introduction to the more detailed discussion of examples and illustrations that follows in the next chapter. These will fill out the analysis by providing a fund of empirical materials that both underline the definition of the types outlined in this chapter and also indicate the rich variation that exists within the types.

Summary

- Types of control range along a continuum between healthy and pathological forms.
- At the 'healthier' end are those involving mutual benign control and those that include 'soft' manipulative elements. Also, 'positional' control as it exists in many social organizations is to be found in this part of the spectrum.
- The pathological types of control include harder manipulation and exploitation like emotional blackmail, the authoritarian control of repressive political regimes, and the dominative-exploitative forms exemplified in women abuse and serial murder.

5

Familiar Issues and Examples

Preview

- This chapter expands on the discussion in the previous one on 'types and dimensions' by drawing on familiar examples from everyday life.
- The links between intimacy and benign control are illustrated by examples taken from the areas of love and romance, female sexual pleasure and family ties.
- The topic of work and careers highlights the question of positional control as well as emotional labour and career systems as mechanisms of surveillance and control.
- The more manipulative side of interpersonal control is reflected in addictive love or co-dependence, emotional terrorism and emotional blackmail.
- Malign, exploitative control is exemplified by repressive positional control, women abuse and serial murder.

How do the types of control manifest themselves in commonly observed features of everyday life? The discussion begins with an examination of the general nature of intimacy as a prime example of benign control. In everyday life we tend to think of intimacy as incompatible with control. It is as if to think of it in control terms would be to crush the raw essence of feelings and spontaneity associated with intimacy. However, if the nature of intimacy is closely scrutinized, it becomes apparent that it can really only be achieved via mutual control and influence over each other's feelings and interests. Intimacy depends on the ability to elicit someone's trust, openness and vulnerability. In this sense the creation of intimacy requires the skilled and sensitive use of benign control and influence.

Intimacy does not simply 'happen' as the result of some instinctive process of mutual attraction, although 'instinct' and intuition may play a part initially in drawing people together. Intimacy has to be created through the efforts and 'negotiated' agreements of those involved. To be intimate, people have to 'open up' emotionally and be vulnerable to each other, and this requires trust. However, trust is only possible when it is accompanied by sincerity; only then do we feel safe enough to confide in each other.

Trust of this kind may be formed in but a few hours of meeting someone for the first time, or it may require months (or longer) to develop. However long it takes, a willingness to trust each other 'emerges' out of the communication between those involved. They have to persuade each other by conversation, argument, behaviour, expressed feelings and attitudes that they are indeed trustworthy. In other words, intimacy has to be earned and achieved through interpersonal contact over time. Until this happens, individuals may remain guarded about their vulnerabilities and even attempt to conceal them. Trust and vulnerability, then, are preludes to intimacy.

Moreover, the emotional underpinnings of self-identity (basic security, self-esteem, efficacy and control) are never achieved or 'resolved' once and for all. Since intimacy itself is closely involved with identity issues, its 'attainment' must be viewed in a similar way. In short, the creation of intimacy must be understood as a continuous accomplishment of situated behaviour.

Romance, Love and Power

The very nature of love itself seems to stress qualities of tenderness, caring, emotional rapport, connectedness and so on, all of which seem antithetical to power and control. But in fact the issue of control enters deeply into emotional expression, and love and romance are no exceptions. This is reflected, for example, in the desire of a lover to be loved equally in return, or in the priority given to the loved one in practical decisions, career moves, physical and emotional satisfaction and so forth. Although lovers' conversations are frequently about such matters (often ending in lovers' tiffs or spats), they are rarely explicitly about the underlying balance of power. Indeed, as Ethel Person (1990) points out, a happy and stable relationship is one based on a workable balance of power that operates silently, behind the scenes, and may be largely unnoticed or unremarked by the partners themselves. In fact, unless one of them feels unsatisfied, unfairly treated or exploited, the partners may remain blissfully unaware of the 'true' state of the power balance. However, if the relationship is already in a bad way, the partners may become locked into a struggle for power. Mutual giving, caring and self-sacrifice may degenerate into the raw need to 'take' more, in order to avoid feeling cheated.

Of course, all intimate relationships go through highs and lows and are constantly evolving. A seemingly 'good' or 'perfect' relationship may be shattered by the infidelity or disloyalty of one of the partners, giving rise to resentments and squabbles about being 'used' or exploited. For the wronged partner, a threatened or actual break-up may make it important to regain some control and this may lead to vengeful attempts to 'get even'. But regardless of how 'obvious' or visible it is, control is at the heart of any romantic bond. Lovers not only feel the need to 'surrender' themselves to their loved one, to be selflessly enthralled by them, but also in a special way, they want to 'possess' their lover. Unfortunately these desires pull in opposite directions.

Possession of a lover, in this sense, entails having more or less exclusive rights to their time, energy and most intimate feelings. But of course, this restricts the freedom of the loved one and this is alien to the spirit and nature of genuine love. Manipulating and restricting the loved one will likely prevent them from giving their love freely and spontaneously. The project of 'possession', therefore, is doomed to failure because in a certain sense love is 'of the soul' and cannot simply be appropriated or stolen by another. Thus the freely given, emotionally positive 'essence' of love can never be 'possessed'. Any attempt to capture it by disregarding the feelings and intentions of the love 'object' is unrealistic and can only thwart the emergence of genuine love.

This basic lover's dilemma can give rise to a number of relationship problems. For instance, mild possessiveness due to jealousy or insecurity may eventually become oppressive and unhealthy. The more vulnerable an individual is, in this regard, the more likely is it that they will become dependent and fear rejection. In turn, this may create resentment and lead to emotional manipulation (or even physical abuse) as a means of regaining or maintaining control. This, of course, merely creates greater unhappiness and will make the 'target' partner more resolute about abandoning the relationship.

On the other hand, a lover may use 'submissiveness' as a tactic for 'getting their way' in the relationship. This may be because they actually are in a weaker position, but in some cases it may be a ploy designed to create dependence in their partner. As Person points out, this can involve sexual seduction, flattery or placing the other's needs before one's own. Unfortunately, submissiveness can be damaging for self-esteem and as a result, the submissive partner may start having affairs in order to boost their confidence and to 'get even'. Overall, neither manipulation nor submission works as a long-term strategy because the 'love' is based on false foundations and this typically leads to mutual anger, resentment or aggression.

Another facet of the lover's dilemma is associated with the fact that love meets the need to overcome loneliness by blocking it out with an intense emotional bond. However, the very intensity of the bond may prove to be a problem in its own right. While the exclusivity and blending together of two people meet the need for togetherness and involvement, taken to an extreme this can easily 'flip over' into feelings of entrapment or suffocation.

If neither partner is given enough room for independence, they may begin to feel stifled and resentful. Typically, a person who is restricted in this manner will try to engineer some breathing space by creating (emotional) distance in the relationship. But because the partner is already insecure and vulnerable, the strategy of emotional distancing may cause even more anxiety. These possibilities suggest a shift in the balance of control between partners towards a more unhealthy arrangement. This simply highlights the riskiness and uncertainty inherent in all relationships. In so far as relationships are changeable and always 'in process', they may be experienced as fragile and unpredictable in nature.

This core feature of mutual benign control highlights the mixed motive basis of human behaviour involving a subtle and complex blend of selfishness and altruism. Intimacy can go wrong if it is not 'worked at' on a relatively continuous basis. It is always moving into and out of a state of 'balance' agreed upon by the partners implicitly or explicitly, on the basis of their overall emotional satisfaction with the relationship.

Perhaps the main criterion by which the health of a loving relationships can be measured is by what Eric Fromm in *The Art of Loving* (1971) describes as the extent to which both partners respect and foster each other's individuality, integrity and personal growth. There has to be a balance between taking your own and your partner's feelings into account. Each person must feel broadly satisfied with what they are giving to, and receiving from, the relationship – especially in terms of emotional and general psychological rapport. Although this may not always entail complete equality, neither partner must feel unduly exploited overall.

Sexual Pleasure and Control

Physical and sensual intimacy is centrally involved in sexual pleasure. As with other kinds of intimacy, sexual pleasure is commonly associated with freedom and spontaneity – a far cry from the restraints normally associated with 'control'. But control is not simply about preventing things from happening – such as not allowing your child to go out unaccompanied, or through self-control by curbing your tendency to become angry. Of course, sometimes control *is* concerned with prevention or prohibition, but it often *enables* people to do things. For instance, overcoming a socially debilitating inhibition such as shyness, or disapproval of a particular sexual practice, can set a person free from self-imposed limitations on enjoyment. Self-mastery of this kind is not concerned with closing down areas of freedom but is rather about opening up previously 'forbidden' opportunities. Furthermore, overcoming an inhibition such as chronic shyness will, more than likely, enable the person to exert more control and influence over others.

The expansion of personal possibilities through control is pertinent to sexual pleasure. Rachel Swift (1994) underlines the importance of control in women's subjective experience of sexual enjoyment. She cites examples of women who find it difficult to achieve orgasm even with male sexual partners whom they find physically attractive. However, these same women can bring themselves to orgasm quickly and easily through masturbation. Swift argues that their inability to achieve sexual pleasure with men friends has to do with experiencing an 'invisible barrier' – otherwise described as a 'loss of control'. She claims that this is not related to a technical difference between masturbation and sex with their partner. Rather, it reflects the difference between having 'total' rather than partial control over the situation. In short, Swift argues that women's sexual pleasure is dependent on the experience of control in the bedroom.

The more the woman feels 'in control' rather than 'controlled by' the man, the more she will experience satisfying sex. Clearly this is related to a wider argument about inequality between the sexes and the widely held assumption that men should be, or generally are thought to be, the active and dominant partners. They are expected to take the initiative in sexual matters, while women are generally expected to be passive and submissive. Clearly, the experience of true sexual pleasure is about overcoming these stereotypes. It depends on achieving a balance between partners in sexual activity so that both feel a sense of control.

Swift defines this as a feeling of complete control, of total ease about one's sexual aims. Importantly, in this context, control is not with regard to your partner, but with 'yourself and your partnership' (1994: 36). According to Swift, many women lose control in the bedroom without realizing it. With a view to helping women regain control, she identifies two types. 'Visible control' refers to control over the body and its responses and involves refusing to 'lie back' and let the man take charge. Crucially, it requires that the woman actively 'shows' the man what she wants with regard to what she finds pleasurable.

'Invisible control' is far more subtle and difficult to pin down since it refers to a state of mind. Taking control in this sense includes coming to grips with vague feelings of submissiveness in the sexual arena, despite having a generally liberated attitude to gender matters. This entails encouraging the woman not to feel duty-bound to place the man's needs before her own; dealing with feelings of being the 'prey' and under the scrutiny of men; coming to terms with (often imagined) fears that her partner will reject her after so many years. Taking control in these invisible areas allows a woman to be free to relax and enjoy personally satisfying sex.

According to Swift, the myth of the passive, submissive woman is very pervasive in modern culture and is reflected in films and romantic fiction. This myth should be challenged if women are to achieve more control and full sexual satisfaction in the bedroom. However, it is important not to confuse the idea of being active and controlling with being 'loud, aggressive and unfeminine'. According to Swift, being strong, knowing what you want sexually and communicating it, can be very attractive and appealing to men. Swift suggests that 'quiet insistence, or refusal to give in or compromise' (1994: 47) is often most effective. Moreover, there is evidence to suggest that this, in fact, is what more and more men want. The Hite report on Male Sexuality reports interviews with men in which a large number complain that women are too passive. Only a handful of men said they always preferred to be the 'aggressors', most wished that women would take the initiative and make the first advance. This strongly suggests that men prefer women to show a degree of control in sexual matters.

Swift's discussion draws attention to the close tie between intimacy and control in sexual encounters. Women (and I would argue men also) must have some level of control in order to obtain complete sexual satisfaction and this highlights the links between self-control, empowerment and benign control over others. Intimacy has to be negotiated and attained by a quiet but firm 'assertiveness', which involves guiding, showing or otherwise communicating to the other what he or she wants in the way of physical stimulation.

To do this, women have to break down the 'invisible' psychological barrier of submissiveness or passivity, or the feeling that their own sexual fulfilment should take second place to that of men. Although Swift doesn't say this, I would argue that this kind of analysis applies equally to men. Men typically struggle with the often unwanted and burdensome 'responsibility' of always being the ones 'expected' to initiate sexual activity or to always be the active (rather than the passive) one. Feeling compelled to conform to such stereotypical behaviour is debilitating regardless of gender. Avoiding the more constraining aspects of social and cultural expectations pinpoints the role of discourse here. In this sense people are always at liberty to choose their behaviour, in this case to reject stereotypes, and the conformist behaviour they entail. That is, individuals are ultimately free to reject, modify or reshape the discourses that are relevant to their circumstances and to integrate them into their behaviour as they see fit.

Emotions and Personal Qualities

There is a diverse array of emotions, feelings and personal qualities associated with both the mutual and manipulative forms of benign control. But they are also related to the kinds of social settings commonly linked with them. Families, friendships, romantic and sexual partnerships hold many possibilities for the expression of particular kinds of emotion and feeling. They also reflect the characteristic 'mixing' of manipulative and mutual benign control.

Typical family relationships provide striking examples of these issues. The public face of the family, of course, stresses its essentially benign nature. It is often portrayed as the most important forum for intimacy and is frequently 'claimed' as a haven of love, security, emotional nourishment and support. While such emotions and feeling states are often found in family settings, real life so often demonstrates that the family can also be the natural home and point of origin of 'negative' emotional experiences. Where love is at a premium and keenly contested, there will also exist the possibility of its withdrawal, or its degeneration into bickering, arguments and resentment. Consequently pain, hurt and disappointment are also frequently to be found at the heart of the family.

This 'darker' side of family bonds remains largely unacknowledged since it represents a 'private interior world' that impinges only on the lived experience of those actually involved. These same individuals sometimes even suppress or edit out such experiences from their public pronouncements. None the less, the actual fabric of family life – the bonds, obligations and responsibilities that are implicit in relationships between members – is usually characterized by an uneven mixture of mutually benign and manipulative-benign forms of control and the positive and negative emotions that accompany them.

A good example of the normally 'shrouded' darker side of the inner life of family ties is exemplified in the public disclosures of Princess Diana's 'private' butler after her death. Paul Burrell's revelations not only exposed the continual feuding and bitterness between the Windsor and the Spencer families, but also laid bare the jealousies, bitterness and resentments between individuals within each of the families both before Diana's death and long after it. It transpires that Diana and her mother Frances Shand Kydd, had a bitter argument about Diana's choice of men friends and sexual partners. According to Burrell, her mother's angry disapproval and her own refusal to acquiesce evidently caused much hurt and unhappiness. Burrell alleges that Diana was further alienated from her blood family by her brother's refusal to let her stay at a cottage on his (the Spencer) estate so that she could use it as a bolt hole from the pressures of public life. Lord Spencer's subsequent eulogy of his sister at her funeral struck Burrell as the height of hypocrisy, given that he clearly disapproved of her behaviour in life and what he felt she represented.

Finally, Burrell revealed that Diana's sister was extremely jealous of her, particularly her marriage into royalty and resented the power and riches she had acquired as a result. All in all, Burrell contends that before her death, Diana felt painfully estranged from, and – for all practical purposes – rejected by, her blood family. Her family, for their part, regarded her as a 'dangerous' renegade and made her the target of unrelenting criticism, emotional abuse and attempted manipulation.

There is nothing remarkable about these disclosures in the sense that they are common to many family circumstances. Aristocratic families are no more protected from such pathologies of intimacy than are any others. The disclosures simply underline the ubiquity of the darker elements of family life, normally kept hidden from public scrutiny. In Diana's case she experienced strained relations and was subjected to behaviour that involved manipulative-exploitative types of control. It is clear that once soured or wounded relationships have become chronically entrenched in antagonisms and alliances between family members, there is little left of 'healthy' mutual benign control. What makes control benign in an overall sense is the tendency for strained and imbalanced relations quickly to return to normal. Typically those involved in benign control are reluctant to stray beyond the normal limits of 'soft' (non-exploitative) manipulation as a means of managing ongoing problems. Much of Diana's family's behaviour towards her was 'pathological'. Rifts between mothers and daughters, fathers and sons, spouses or partners may rapidly become impossible to contain within the boundaries of benign control.

Communication and Distortions of Intimacy

Family antagonisms or parental disapproval of potential romantic and marital partners are common to all families regardless of class or status. Long-standing disputes and 'harboured' feelings between siblings, or between parents and offspring about interference or 'meddling' are the stock-in-trade of families the world over. As a result, they can easily lead to entrenched bitterness, hurt and pain, instead of the love, security and support that is expected of such 'primary' bonds. The 'pathologizing' of these relationships is reflected in the degree to which deception, self-interest and manipulation come to play a prominent role. Emotional blackmail and harassment are common features of relationships that have 'gone bad' in this manner.

But this is a key point. Although such unhealthy ways of relating have, as it were, reached a qualitatively different stage of development, there is nevertheless an element of continuity between healthy and unhealthy types. The question of intimacy lies at the heart of the issue and exploitative manipulation is usefully thought of as a 'distorted' version of intimacy. It is a way of preserving the nominal outward appearance of intimacy while rejecting those basic qualities normally linked with it, such as altruism, honesty sincerity, empathy, fidelity and so forth.

Work and Positional Control

In more formal settings like those of work, 'disclosing intimacy' (Jamieson 1998; Giddens 1984) is more often than not an 'added extra' imported from informal settings. This is because positional control predominates in these settings, and while employees and managers are encouraged 'to get to know each other', the primary purpose of such injunctions is to facilitate the smooth functioning of the work organization itself. Thus mutual benign control is displaced by the more dominant influence of position-practices. The sincerity and trust at the core of mutual benign control are shunted into the background of interpersonal dealing while those features that facilitate the co-operation of the workforce through employer control (Edwards 1979), take precedence. But this is not, as Habermas (1984, 1987) claims, an all or nothing process in which system values and imperatives invade and colonize whole segments of the life-world. There is never a total separation between personal and positional control for reasons already outlined and as a consequence, their particular influences often 'leak into' each other.

Hochschild's (1983) work throws light on the links between work, emotion and intimacy. She suggests that many work settings require 'emotional labour' and her own study of flight attendants is an excellent example. For flight attendants it is a company requirement that they engage emotionally with passengers. They are encouraged to look upon the cabin as if it were their own sitting room, and to treat the passengers with the same level of emotional-psychological care, understanding and attention as they would members of their own family.

Hochschild points out that in occupations requiring face-to-face communication (between workers and customers or professional and clients), emotional labour is an essential part of the job. School teaching, nursing, social work and so on require different kinds and levels of emotional labour and Hochschild argues that this becomes built into the employer–employee relationship.

Jobs that rely on high levels of emotional labour (as with flight attendants) require employees to simulate pleasant or charming personas or sensitive, caring behaviour irrespective of how they are really feeling or whether they are dealing with a particularly difficult or irate customer. This raises the question of authenticity in relationships and feelings about the self. If there is company pressure to simulate feelings of warmth and caring, even under the most trying of conditions, then a person is more likely to achieve this via deep acting skills rather than by a sincere expression of true or real feelings.

Habermas's thesis about colonization of the life-world by social system pressure needs to be somewhat refined in relation to jobs requiring emotional labour. In these jobs it is not simply that system pressures – as they are mediated through company demands – drive out the benign control and mutual support systems to be found in informal settings. Formal and informal settings do not necessarily compete with each other for a person's time. Although sometimes they do compete, more often in modern society work and family life (or leisure time) are segregated from each other in time and space. Also, individuals always import elements to make the time go more quickly (as in Roy's 1973 study), or to subvert or resist the organizational rules. Such strategies can impact on informal conduct in the workplace, either to make positive or negative effects on efficiency and productivity. Furthermore, communication at the workplace always requires elements of personalized control, even though there is a formal hierarchy of positions and statuses. Personnel skills or 'human resource management' skills are increasingly required to allow the control system to work with maximal efficiency.

Finally, Hochschild's idea that many jobs require emotion work normally found in informal settings, suggests that rather than driving out genuine intimacy altogether, 'the system' in the guise of the company, transmutes and co-opts such life-world elements for its own ends. The real issue is how much, and what type of emotional labour is required in particular jobs and how much sincerity and real feelings are impinged upon, or damaged as a result.

Work and Impersonal Control

In management careers and the work experiences of many blue-collar employees, work lives are lived out under the indirect scrutiny of hierarchical and bureaucratic forms of organization. In these circumstances the requirements for emotional labour are minimized. Although simulated emotion is an intrinsic part of the 'successful' performance of the job, a variety of emotions enter interpersonal relations in rather more subtle ways that are not directly monitored by bosses or superordinates. For example, resistance to incorporation into the company ethos, and reluctance to become personally or emotional committed to the employing organization, are the most likely areas in which these emotions are expressed. But anger, hostility, bitterness and other negative feelings associated with disapproval of work practices and conditions must be largely suppressed, in order not to attract attention or incur penalties for flouting company rules.

Middle managers and senior managers themselves have a typical spread of emotional responses depending on their specific career circumstances. The more they believe they are high-flyers and key individuals in ensuring the firm's future fortunes, the more strongly will they be loyal and committed to the employing company. On the other hand, the more they have been 'passed over' for promotion, and become 'too old' for a move into the senior echelons, the more disappointed, bitter and frustrated they will feel. The career system, a typical feature of such employing organizations, is the key to securing the individual's attachment to it.

A person's loyalty, commitment and positive attitude towards the company rest squarely on how much the initial incentive of career progression (proffered at the beginning of the career) has actually been translated into work (and social) success and status. The more the individual feels left behind in career terms, the more she or he will begin to lose faith in the early promises held out for progression through the company status hierarchy. But the quality of an individual's attachment and commitment is also reflected in responses to their current work situation – measured in terms of how they get on with colleagues, superiors and subordinates.

Being able to work with particular colleagues, and trusting and accepting the authority of seniors, is often dependent on whether the individual feels 'psychologically embraced' by the company in terms of deserved career rewards. As Peters and Waterman (1995) have highlighted, the quality of an individual's bond with an employing organization is revealed in how 'significant' he or she feels (in terms of their value and contribution) to that organization. It is hard for an employee not to measure 'significance' or personal value as reflected in their achievement of career rewards.

Manipulating Feelings: Emotional Abuse

In benign control, even where self-interest begins to threaten the subtle balance between altruism and egoism, excessive self-serving is reined back by self-awareness and the desire to do the right thing. This is the dividing line between 'healthy', benign control and the more pathological forms in which altruism is quashed and self-interest takes precedence. In this sense true exploitative manipulation comes to play a predominant role. Benign control is never eradicated entirely but is, rather, transmuted into pathological forms. Pathological control is erected on the foundation of benign control because it is a necessary precondition of manipulation and exploitation. Because they need to employ benign control in 'other' facets of their lives, habitual users of pathological control often use benign control to disguise their anti-social tendencies. But some forms of manipulation and exploitation actually depend on an underlay of benign control for their effectiveness.

In informal settings involving families, friendships and romantic partnerships, there is great scope not only for mutual benign control, but also for emotional manipulation and feelings traps. Although such relationships may have a smooth and harmonious outward appearance, this may mask long-standing strains and tensions. Relationships normally involve a degree of struggle and conflict. Unresolved problems may cause an initially 'healthy' relationship to be gradually transformed into a manipulative and exploitative one. What was once a straightforward romantic liaison may turn into an unhealthily 'addictive' relationship. Over the long term, uplifting emotional ties between family members may lead to suffocating concern or burdensome guilt. In situations like these, the normal element of mutual benign control has gone wrong in some way. A once healthy, thriving relationship has deteriorated into a sick and oppressive one.

In some cases apparently healthy intimate relationships were never really healthy in the first place. The strange or unreasonable behaviour of one or both the partners may have been disguised or lying dormant until the right conditions trigger a 'pathological' response. In such examples the shared satisfaction of the partners is sacrificed for the self-interest of the dominant one. A seemingly dominant partner may feel threatened by the other's independence, or fear that they will abandon them. In this sense the 'pathological' control strategy is in response to a loss, or threatened loss of control in intimate ties.

Addictive Love and Co-dependence

Addictive love (Peele and Brodsky 1974) or 'co-dependence' signifies relationships in which lovers are so dependent and focused on each other that they exclude other people from their social world. This kind of arrangement 'attracts' individuals who are already personally insecure. Their anxiety makes them uneasy about allowing a lover any independent interests or relationships outside the pair bond. Such individuals are driven to seek lovers who will allow themselves to be 'taken over' and completely possessed, but at the same time will also preoccupy and absorb them. The separate lives of both partners are relinquished for the sake of a very close, almost suffocating relationship that seems to offer them a defence against loneliness and anxiety. Unfortunately, such an arrangement only creates a mutually imposed 'prison' that can barely contain the underlying tensions in the relationship.

In practical terms addictive, mutual dependence means that the lovers virtually live out of each other's pockets, spending all their time together focused on mutual psychological needs and neglecting previous friendships and ties. Other people are considered 'an intrusion' which may threaten the security and solidarity of the relationship. In time, the relationship itself becomes exclusive, providing the only psychological support, companionship and source of self-esteem for both lovers. Of course, this restricts the personal growth and independence of both partners – the opposite of 'healthy love' according to Fromm (1971).

A potentially volatile situation is thus created. If time spent with other people and activities external to the relationship is seen as threatening to it, the partners need to prevent these things from happening. They each must ensure that the other sticks rigidly to the 'rule' that emotional support will not be sought outside the confines of the relationship and thus both parties need to closely monitor each other's behaviour. As a result of intense mutual surveillance, the relationship may become suffocating and intolerable.

If anything disturbs the existing status quo in the bond, then the fragility of the 'arrangement' may become all too apparent. The partners might feel oppressed by the claustrophobic atmosphere and begin to look for greater independence outside the relationship. A woman who has been restricted to housework may get a job or go to university. A man may go out socializing without his partner. Assertions of independence like this may prove threatening to the other partner who may thus become hostile and resistant.

Mutual over-dependence is clearly unhealthy 'intimacy'. However, the opposite extreme whereby partners lead entirely separate lives, barely engaging with each other emotionally, is hardly any healthier. Fromm (1971) has suggested that a 'healthy' relationship is one that allows individuals to pursue separate interests as well as enjoying time together. To enable a partner to grow and develop (as an individual), their contact with other people must not be limited. However, allowing mutual freedom requires each person to be secure about themselves in the first place. If this is so, neither of them will need to resort to over-control for fear of losing their partner. But this is the central problem of addictive love or co-dependence. Both lovers attempt to control each other's behaviour because they are unsure of their own individuality. They are secure only as a couple and this ensures their mutual over-dependence.

Emotional Terrorism

In co-dependence there is a shared responsibility for the problems in the relationship. In emotional terrorism, by contrast, the domination of one partner's agenda creates the instability. They construct a regime in which their partner lives in constant fear of their unpredictable outbursts. Although some tyrants use physical and psychological means to get what they want, the pure emotional terrorist relies primarily on psychological cruelty. Chronic insecurity is the basis of a lack of respect and trust in their partner which leads to manipulation and control. Rather than punishing themselves for their own failings (like insecurity) through self-hate or depression, the terrorist turns rage and moodiness outwards towards the person who is most vulnerable or close at hand.

Susan Stewart (1998) documents five years of married life with a man who was an emotional terrorist. Before marriage she thought of her future husband as a gentle, warm and intelligent man, but after two months of marriage she says he had become a 'cold manipulative bully'. Quite unpredictably he would fly into rages over what can only be termed trivial domestic details of life, blaming his wife totally for what he claimed were her failings and mistakes. One such incident in which he claimed she had not matched his socks properly was greeted with a vicious flash of temper and followed by two weeks of silent rage.

Stewart describes his emotional bullying as regularly involving 'protracted sulking silences' and suggests that this is typical where the terrorist combines utter contempt with a strong dependency and a chronic fear of losing his (or her) partner. Her husband's silence was a powerful method of gaining control over the relationship in order to allay his own insecurity. In this respect, Stewart conjectures that his insecurity had been a result of his father's bullying, which had also included his mother. He felt inferior to his wife and, as a consequence, wanted to have her 'under his thumb'.

Stewart herself suggests that initially trying to appease and mollify her husband was mistaken because it simply encouraged the cycle of psychological bullying to continue. It also undermined her own self-esteem because she began to believe that she was indeed what he angrily accused her of being – a 'stupid bitch' or 'mad'. Clearly this man's festering insecurity and inferiority meant that he could not tolerate even the slightest indication that he was not in complete control of the situation. His emotional bullying was thus a vain attempt to pre-empt any shift in power or loss of control in the relationship. The combination of extreme rage and sulking silences was way of externalizing and denying his own failures.

This type of emotional terrorism involves a subtle combination of psychological manipulation with the implied threat of physical intimidation – although in this case, mental torture rather than physical violence was the main weapon. However, emotional bullying remains, in fact, a rather blunt means of asserting control in a relationship. All the subtle lures and gentle enticements of mutual benign control are simply ignored. In this respect emotional terrorism differs from emotional blackmail in which more complex psychological pressures are brought to bear on potential victims.

Emotional Blackmail

Although subtler than emotional terrorism, emotional blackmail is, nevertheless, manipulative and exploitative. The extent to which benign control is involved depends on whether the blackmail is high-pressure and confrontational, or low-key and behind the scenes. High pressure means that there is less room for subtlety and a greater tendency for bullying. But the objective of the emotional blackmailer is always the same: to obtain someone's compliance by the actual or threatened withdrawal of emotional support such as love or approval.

As Forward and Fraser (1998: 13) observe, many of the people who use emotional blackmail are 'friends, colleagues and family members with whom we have close ties that we want to strengthen and salvage'. But it is this closeness that is abused by the blackmailer, since he or she uses intimate knowledge of a person's deepest personal secrets in order to make them compliant. Intimacy, therefore, is always an artifice or ruse created to entrap the victim. The blackmailer exploits the need for love and approval by threatening to withhold them altogether and aims to make the target feel that care, love and approval need to be 'earned' by submission and compliance.

A person's fears, secrets and vulnerabilities are drawn into the game. If, for instance, someone believes that they are generous and caring, the blackmailer will turn this around and accuse them of selfishness. 'How could you be so selfish after all I've done for you' is a typical ploy that generates obligation and fear in the target. The fact that the target is emotionally committed to the relationship makes this an even more insidious and compelling strategy.

Forward and Fraser suggest that blackmailers appear in four typical guises. Each employs a different vocabulary with which to threaten, demand and pressurize their potential victims. '*Punishers*' are clear about what they want and the implications that will follow if they don't get it. They may express themselves aggressively as in 'If you try to divorce me you'll never see the kids again'. Alternatively, they may 'smoulder in silence' (1998: 41) and deflect any responsibility for their own feelings on to the target (reminiscent of emotional terrorism). Parents are often punishers in this sense by making their children 'choose between them and other people they love, setting up a situation in which any choice is seen as a betrayal' (1998: 46).

'*Self-punishers*' turn their threats inward, stressing what they will do to themselves if they don't get their way, for example, by threatening to damage their own health or happiness. This is reflected in such responses as 'Don't argue with me or I'll get sick or depressed' or 'If you leave me I'll kill myself'. The third variety, the '*sufferers*', don't threaten to harm themselves or the target but let it be known that 'If you don't do what I want, I will suffer and it will be your fault'. This is the case when a mother responds to her son or daughter's telephone call with an accusation that she might as well be dead for all they really care.

The final type, the '*tantalizers*', put victims through a never-ending series of tests and demands promising material rewards such as money or a promotion or less tangible things such as love and acceptance, if only the victim will give them what they want. Every offer, however, has strings attached to it and the succession of hoops and demands never ceases. The endless game of lures, promises and 'incentives' is an effective means of control. As with the other types, tantalizers may combine different types of blackmail and switch back and forth between them, making control over their victims more extensive and effective.

Emotional blackmailers are similar to emotional terrorists in that their desperate need to control others is born out of some inadequacy or failure in themselves. Insecurity about their ability to attract and keep love and approval, or a fear of abandonment by their loved one, drives them to exert an inappropriate level of control over some of their closest friends, family or colleagues. However, the blackmailer is typically less of a monster than the terrorist. He or she is less moved by malice or hatred than by insecurity and fear. Without doubt the emotional terrorist is likewise fearful and insecure, but this inner 'weakness' is somehow transformed into an aggressive hatred of the person who is the object of their tyranny. Unfortunately, the victims of emotional blackmail, like those of emotional terrorism, simply refuel the cycle of oppressive control by giving in to it.

The Darker Side of Intimacy

Some 'normal' parental control over children may include milder kinds of emotional manipulation – such as embarrassing a child in front of his or her friends – in order to stop them 'being naughty' or to make them 'behave properly'. But parents who themselves may be somewhat maladjusted can also exert more sinister kinds of control over their offspring. Here, the division between healthy and unhealthy control may become blurred.

While parents obviously must bring their children up in the manner they think is 'right', this doesn't always guarantee that the children will turn out to be properly adjusted. Often parental control has a deleterious effect on the child's ability to learn or to become emotionally independent. The 'normal' reluctance of parents to let their children 'leave the nest' may easily become distorted into an attempt to tie them permanently to the family (or a particular parent) by the use of control strategies that induce fear (of abandonment), guilt and obligation.

Parents who clearly exert an unhealthy level of control over their children have some fairly explicit agenda (even if denied or unspoken) about preventing the family's 'private business' coming into contact with the wider world. Although healthy families act less consciously and deliberately as guardians of some 'inner secret', they none the less often regard 'family business' (loyalties to kin, emotional commitments and shared experiences) as sacrosanct. In this sense, family commitments are felt to be more binding and important than external friendships or relationships with work colleagues and so on. Within this space, family members are bound by the implicit understandings and expectations that have emerged from the shared 'private history' of the family itself. In such contexts it is clear that intimacy can never be completely pure and uncomplicated. Family members' relationships with outsiders are always in danger of coming into conflict with the obligations and emotional ties of family membership.

The fuzzy nature of the distinction between healthy and unhealthy family environments can in principle be extended to all the supposedly 'close' or emotionally charged relationships that have been discussed under the rubric of emotional manipulation or abuse. It is relatively easy for a relationship that starts life healthily to evolve or become transformed into one that is abnormal or unhealthy. To manipulate someone's feelings and emotions, the 'perpetrator' must build on a solid basis of benign control. The manipulator must have a solid grip on the inner emotional life of the 'target' and this can only be achieved by obtaining their trust through deception. Once revealed, inner secrets, emotional vulnerabilities, patterns of shame and guilt may be used against the person as a means of control.

Repressive Control

The pathological 'equivalent' of positional control in work settings is typically tied to political repression. In such regimes 'authority' and the positions, statuses and practices associated with them are not legitimately underpinned by consent. Rather, authority is based on the raw arrogation of power through the use of force. Repressive authority is based on a command principle in which orders flow downwards in a hierarchical fashion.

Subordinates are not expected to use their personal discretion but to obey unquestioningly, otherwise they will be disciplined and punished. Repressive authority is strictly hierarchical, and discipline is based on fear of punishment. Of course, for those who are fully committed to the regime there are positive incentives similar to those found in legitimate systems of authority, such as pay and career progression with their attendant material and psychological rewards. Loyalty to the employing company is replaced by loyalty to the regime or the leader, but is rewarded similarly. For those who are loyal and committed, this kind of system can inspire love and devotion in its adherents, but this is always tempered by the knowledge that if they step out of line or question the authority of the leader or the regime, then repressive punishments will ensue. Thus fear and anxiety about personal commitment to the regime always reside in the background of 'apparent' consent or commitment.

Women Abuse

Women abuse is intermediary between emotional terrorism on the one hand and forms of violent crime on the other. Women abuse in the domestic environment involves the combination of a man's psychological abuse (emotional and verbal) and physical violence in order to control his partner. Sandra Horley (2000: 13) has suggested that often such men are outwardly very charming and able 'to make a woman feel special', but ultimately the charm is used as a disguise to cover up his domination and physical abuse.

Although the terrorism is a very visible part of the living hell that his partner has to endure, the abuse itself is not necessarily visible or obvious to anyone else outside the relationship. One reason is the man's surface 'charm', which makes it difficult for others to detect abuse. Also, these men typically threaten their partners with more violence if they tell others or attempt to get the police involved. Thus, this kind of exploitative control may remain a terrible 'shared' secret enforced by threats and intimidation. As Horley emphasizes, for these and other reasons it is often very difficult for abused women to leave their partners. Paradoxically 'women in this situation often feel less frightened staying with their abusers than if they leave them' (2000: 61).

Women abuse highlights the combined use of different strategies of control. Clearly the man's charm is designed to confuse and deceive his partner (and others), and its success depends on the man's knowledge of and ability to use benign control. His charm has to be 'convincing' and thus it must appear to be genuinely benign. The abuser creates uncertainty, confusion and anxiety in the woman, especially when he alternates the charm with bouts of emotional and physical violence. His very unpredictability and volatility add to the atmosphere of terror.

Although the victim of domination or repression will always have some way of fighting back, this is usually not enough to alter their situation. Where fear, intimidation and frustration are the order of the day, an abuse victim's personal powers are very limited. In common with master–slave or hostage relationships, abused women typically have no other option but to adapt to the situation as a short-term survival strategy.

Horley argues against the accusation that abused women simply give up trying to change the situation and become passive, submissive and helpless. Rather it is their isolation from friends and outside support that prompts their need for survival. As is also the case with hostages, abused women often adopt 'apparently' submissive behaviour as a way of buying 'themselves time while they can think of a long-term strategy or an escape plan'(2000: 88). By adopting short-term survival plans, the women must not be seen as 'pathetic', 'passive victims', but rather as resourceful and coping survivors. In this sense, although it is severely reduced, the woman does retain a minimal area of freedom and resistance.

Stealing Control: the Frissons of Crime

Crime provides a short-cut to control. Control over one's life situation, control over others, control over the perceived 'inequities' that society visits upon us by virtue of our membership. As a short-cut, the potential immediacy of the rewards of crime is paramount for the criminal. It's the opposite of deferred gratification. All the drudgery of patiently waiting, the tiresome effort required by the legitimate routes to success, magically vanish by the simple act of 'taking' things regardless of their ownership. There is also the thrill of the act, the transcendence of conventional morality and law, the frisson of 'taking control'. These elements make crime a most attractive way of dispensing with the psychological burdens that attend the normal and healthier forms of interpersonal control.

Katz (1988) emphasizes what he calls the 'seductions and compulsions' which underpin criminal activities. Thus he draws attention away from 'conventional explanations' of the 'causes' of crime such as ethnicity, poverty and so on. The seizure of power and control in armed robbery or gang violence gratifies the perpetrator's emotional needs for attention, status, excitement and thrills and the venting of moral indignation, rage or humiliation. The expression of such emotion often reflects a desperation to escape from boredom and meaninglessness by 'transcending' the constraints of mundane reality, authority and law.

Where individuals are leading chaotic lives, crime offers a definite focus and the creation of personal meaning by becoming someone to be reckoned with, or a 'star' criminal. This is reflected in the violence of individuals involved in gangs. As Katz suggests, a 'badass' male has to project the idea that he is influenced by no one, but that anyone could be the focus of his attention and control at any time. He has to convince you that he is not from 'your' conventional world but from a place inaccessible to you, which you cannot deal with or control. He does this by projecting an unmitigated meanness and a willingness to explode into violence at any moment – to destroy you and your world. The elusive, unknowable self of the badass thus claims ultimate control of situations and their meanings.

But it matters little whether the emotional impetus for criminal activity is boredom, the search for status or simply creating meaning and excitement in an otherwise dull and empty existence. Crime is a means of achieving immediate control over one's life situation. Moreover, by imposing their desires and meanings on the world, criminals are free to express emotion and control regardless of others' feelings, interests, rights and physical and mental well-being.

Ultimate Control: Serial Murder

Holmes and DeBurger (1998) suggest that serial murders usually only involve two people: the victim and the assailant, who are typically 'strangers' to each other. In this respect they are not crimes of passion, nor are they precipitated by the victim. The murders also seem 'motiveless' except that the obvious intention of the perpetrator is to kill the victim. Finally, serial murders involve a series of repetitive killings that continue until the killer is apprehended – usually between 10 and 12 murders over a period of several years. Serial killers often blend into the community, seeming to be socially responsible, perhaps holding a job and keeping a low profile. They do not give the impression of being insane – such outwards signs would quickly lead to detection and arrest. Because of their low profile and the fact that they choose strangers as victims, serial killers may lead normal, undetected lives for years and their eventual discovery and apprehension may occur by chance.

Holmes and Deburger identify four types of serial killer. The 'visionary' type is likely to be mentally ill and hears voices who instruct him to kill, while the 'missionary' type is usually not mentally disturbed and has a consciously worked-out mission to eliminate a certain group of people, say prostitutes. The 'hedonist' kills for the excitement and pleasure it brings, and this includes lust murder and various kinds of sexual deviation. Finally, the 'power/control' killer derives pleasure from the ability to exert ultimate control over his helpless victim.

Although it is generally useful to distinguish between 'types' like this, it is misleading to suggest that the power/control type is separate or distinct from the others. Clearly, control is an essential feature of all types of serial murderer, although different issues around control may be significant distinguishing characteristics. I am more sympathetic to Canter's (1994) view that it is possible to understand violent criminality in terms of the role the perpetrator assigns his victim, as well as the level of violence and control he uses against them. The victim can be viewed as 'object', 'vehicle' or 'person' – each representing a distortion of intimacy. The levels of violent domination range from the extreme of murder with frenzied mutilation, to violent rape and murder. This approach affirms the importance of different levels of control and the search for distorted intimacy that are present in these types of violent crime.

But it is equally important not to lose sight of the fact that such killers may use both benign and exploitative control to reinforce each other. Benign control can be and often is used selectively, say at work or in home life so as to allow the murderer to 'simulate' normal life and throw a veil over the evil nature of his 'other life' of murderous activity. Second, a serial murderer may routinely use persuasion, enticement and other benign 'inducements' to put his potential victims 'off-guard' prior to the attack.

Both Dennis Nilsen in the UK and Jeffrey Dahmer in the USA made contact with their victims by striking up conversations in bars and even sharing a drink as a 'soothing' prelude to murder. It seems that they were able to move easily between different forms of control (and their vastly different moral underpinnings) in a manner that 'normal' people would find impossible. In this sense control in serial murder is a matter of degree and type not of presence or absence, as Holmes and Deburger seem to imply.

The motives of serial murderers also confirm a solid link between control and social psychological 'problems'. For instance, often the self-identities of such killers are brittle and fragile and this can play a part in the motivation to kill. In his biography of Dennis Nilsen, Brian Masters (1995) argues that Nilsen's homicidal aggression represented a breakdown of self-control and was expressed in order to prevent extensive personality disintegration. Thus murder was a release mechanism that forestalled an even more serious collapse of the self.

Also Hale (1998) has argued that serial murderers are prone to experience humiliation in a heightened manner, even where it doesn't exist. If the killer experiences an early humiliation that attacks their self-worth or self-esteem, it may trigger a vicious criminal act. This overcomes the humiliation and helps the perpetrator regain the lost power whilst also rectifying 'the wrong' to which they have been subjected. Hale suggests the motivational basis of Ted Bundy's murderous rampages in the USA, when Bundy killed as many as 23 young, attractive, white women, was his rejection by a former girlfriend.

Similarly, serial killers often feel detached from others and resentful and bitter that their 'talents' have not been recognized, which reinforces low self-esteem. By becoming an evil killing machine and operating in a totally selfish manner, the serial killer gains a sense of power, status, notoriety or even fame. Some serial murderers (including Henry Lee Lucas, Charles Manson and Ted Bundy in the USA and Dennis Nilson in the UK), believe that they lack the power and influence that they *should* have on the world, and thus become serial killers in an attempt to gain social (albeit negative) significance. It becomes a chilling way of demonstrating their 'specialness' and influence on the world and forces others to take notice.

Linked to the fragility of self-identity and low self-esteem, some serial killers are chronically unable to attract and maintain meaningful relationships. A lack of control over the self is coupled with a felt lack of control over others. These killers are unable to exercise mutual benign control or to make it work successfully for them personally. Jeffrey Dahmer and Dennis Nilsen are clear examples (Masters 1993, 1995). They could not create satisfying responses from others in the way of attraction, intimacy or commitment and thus could not bond with them as human beings.

By committing seemingly pointless and motiveless murders, the individual is responding to the failure to sustain intimacy and fear of abandonment and rejection. Both Dahmer's and Nilsen's sense of inadequacy and powerlessness in ordinary human relationships drove them to adopt desperate and inhuman measures. They killed 'for company', to create the illusion of control and a feeling of effectiveness as human beings. However, each time they tried to simulate a human bond with someone through murder, their sense of failure was further reinforced. Each time they were made to confront the fact that whatever sense of control they gained from taking someone's life was transient, illusory and doomed to fail.

Serial murder is quite distinctive in that in most criminal activities the arrogation of control is simply a means to material and status gains and the emotional rewards attached to them. Certainly, for particular individuals, emotional fixes or additive highs associated with the activity become part of its compelling allure. For the serial murderer, however, control is not merely the means to an end, but the end itself. Control is so tied up with the murderer's psychology, sense of self and experience of life that it is almost impossible to untangle them. He is compelled to act in the way he does in order to assuage a psychological need to control some aspect of himself by exerting ultimate control over the lives of others. Serial killing allows the individual to transform himself from a 'nobody' into someone powerful and important. Although often referred to as 'motiveless', serial murder is, in fact, fuelled by the need to regain control over some aspect of the perpetrator's feelings and daily existence that continually threatens to get out of control.

Conclusion: Types of Interpersonal Control

This and the previous chapter have outlined the full continuum of types of interpersonal control and their typical emotions, feeling states and personal attributes. The continuum ranges from healthy types of control that are a normal and necessary feature of social life to the progressively more pathological ones. The latter are best seen as over-controlling responses to an anticipated loss of power, threats and feelings of powerlessness, or the simple assertion or arrogation of power at the expense of others.

A motif of the discussion has been that there is a continuous thread that connects the more benign and socially necessary forms of control with those that are anti-social in nature – even those that are inhuman or horrific. This thread often traces the transformation and transmutation of benign control into one of its more unhealthy types. In this sense the 'original' benign control has 'failed', and in the process the perpetrator's project has become twisted with the control relationship becoming 'infected' as a consequence.

In other cases, elements of benign control stand, rather uneasily, side by side with those of a more insidious nature, serving as seemingly 'out-of-place' reinforcements to exploitation and domination. But, whatever the case, the pervasiveness and entrenchment of benign and exploitative forms of control in so many familiar areas of everyday life are testaments to the indispensability of control as an intrinsic feature of social life.

Summary

- Intimate relationships are not simply spontaneous creations and expressions of our emotional lives, they have to be worked at, negotiated and achieved.
- The importance of the balance of power in intimate relations is a pivotal feature of love and romantic partnerships and the issue of sexual pleasure.
- Both positive and negative emotions and personal qualities are closely intertwined in these and other relations of intimacy such as family life.
- The area of work provides examples of emotional labour and the emotional responses of individuals to their career experiences and positional control.
- Addictive love or co-dependence, emotional abuse and terrorism and emotional blackmail all represent the darker side of intimacy and the corrosive effects of trying to control others by manipulating and exploiting their feelings.
- Intensely pathological forms of control involve attempts to dominate others. This is reflected in women abuse and, at its most extreme, serial murder.

6

Failures of Control

Preview

- The damaging effects of failures of self-control and control over personal and social relationships.
- Psychological resilience, psychobiography and current life situation.
- Physical and mental illness, stress and feelings of powerlessness.
- Massive control failures and psychotic disorders.
- Crime as an anti-social response to control failure.
- The links between crime and mental disorder.

So far the analysis has proceeded from the point of view of control as a 'successful' or 'positive' accomplishment, even though the pathological types have negative connotations. But, of course, interpersonal relationships are dynamic and ever changing: they are always 'in process'. Thus the degree of control a person actually has is always ebbing and flowing – sometimes in a minor way, but also at times in a more dramatic fashion. The fact that we sometimes experience control raises the question of how individuals deal with failures of control. Success and failure are closely bound together, since the very impulse to control is prompted by the need to deal with problems of uncertainty, anxiety and unpredictability in social interaction as well as obtaining emotional gratification. In so far as our attempts at control fall short in any way, then 'problems' linked with these issues automatically become accentuated.

Chapter 5 dealt with some of the more specific emotions, feeling states and personal attributes that are associated with different types of control, but the question of failure to control and how we deal with it raises more general issues. In short, 'being in control' (and I shall go on to separate out several different meanings of this phrase) is associated with the experience or feeling of happiness in a generic sense, whilst 'being' or 'feeling out of control' is intrinsically linked with unhappiness and misery.

Unpacking these statements a little more, we can say that 'happiness' refers to a variety of feeling states including satisfaction, fulfilment, security, pride and euphoria. It also denotes specific attitudes to life such as whether we regard it as challenging, worthwhile and meaningful. Conversely, 'unhappiness' refers to feelings and experiences like insecurity, confusion, anxiety, shame, embarrassment, unease, disquiet and depression at the meaninglessness and emptiness of life.

Either 'having' (being in) control (of relationships, oneself or one's life) or losing it (being out of control), are pivotal in setting the terms under which emotion and general satisfaction are expressed. In other words, how an individual views his or her current circumstances and future destiny is tightly linked with how they cope with the issue of control in all its guises. Since it is a recurrent and 'routine' problem in social life, how people deal with loss of control will influence their overall sense of happiness and satisfaction with life.

What Is a Loss of Control?

First it is worth distinguishing between what we might call minor or routine losses of control and more significant losses that are more serious in their implications. As we have seen, mutual benign control is characterized by ongoing alterations in the balance of power between those involved. For example, at one point in time, a person may feel that they are (and may actually be) in a 'stronger' position than the other emotionally, materially or in terms of social success or status. This might be because of some alteration of circumstance such as a promotion or other success at work. But equally it may be the result of a subtle change in the emotional basis of the relationship, such as a partner going through a sensitive and vulnerable period in their lives.

Typically though, in mutual benign control such inequalities are not permanent features of the relationship. Power over other aspects of the relationship may mean that the balance is reversed or equalized. Similarly, the changing life circumstances of both partners ensure that alterations in the balance of power never become rigidly fixed. Power is gained and lost in roughly equal measure by both participants so that overall there is an approximate balance in the relationship.

In this sense a normal feature of benign control is that everyone involved will 'suffer' from control loss from time to time on a routine basis. Thus most people learn to handle these losses in a fairly 'routine' manner. They will be unfazed by the loss and realize that it is part of the rough and tumble of such relationships. As soon as one person begins to resent a loss and respond to it by exploitation and manipulation (such as emotional terrorism or blackmail) then it ceases to be mutual or benign.

More serious losses of control, however, have rather different implications. By definition these are not routine. They are critical incidents in which there are significant – and possibly permanent – changes in the balance of power, as for example, in a romantic partnership where one partner falls in love with someone else. For this to have maximum impact on the balance of power, the partner who is 'rejected' must want to counter or reverse the situation because of their continuing feelings for their partner.

In other words, if the 'rejected' one was secretly hoping that their partner would fall in love with someone else in order to be free of what they felt was a dead or stagnant partnership then, in effect, the balance of power in the relationship would be less ruffled. However, if as is often the case, the rejected lover is seriously hurt and surprised by the turn of events, then they face a major power and control loss. More than likely their initial response would be to try to rescue or regain the lost power, say by pleading with their partner, restating how much they love them and emphasizing what shared feelings and experiences will be lost for both of them, and so on.

However, if this is to no avail and the rejecting partner remains adamant and demands a complete break, the rejected one may contemplate other less open and fair dealings such as emotional pressure or blackmail. Alternatively, they may try, emotionally and practically, to accept the loss of the person (and their own power to influence them) and begin to build a new life without them. But as is frequently the case, such an acceptance of loss (and life meaning) may prove impossible, at least in the short-term, and the efforts required in rebuilding their lives may seem insuperable.

The rejected person may respond 'badly' or 'well' to such a control failure. The need to seek revenge in some way may prove to be the overriding impulse. But even this may take a bewildering variety of forms, ranging from destroying personal property to having affairs with their partner's former partners or friends and so on. In short, any counter-strategy might be used as long as it inflicts the maximum 'hurt' on the rejecting partner in return for the hurt they have caused. Whether the rejected person seeks revenge or simply accepts the situation as irreparable and endeavours to get on with their life, a common and underlying reaction would be to experience depression at the loss of their partner and the collapse of shared life meaning that was associated with the partnership.

In this respect depression and other mental disorders can be understood as responses to certain forms of powerlessness. However, it is also important to say that the extent of the depression and its debilitating effects on an individual's life will depend both upon their personal psychobiography and their wider, current life situation. Let us now examine the links between control, control loss and the concept of psychobiography.

Psychobiography

'Psychobiography' denotes the historical emergence of the individual as a social agent. It draws attention to the unique circumstances, experiences and networks of relationships that have significantly formed the individual over time. As such, it 'summarizes' the specific pattern of social and psychological experiences that have produced their unique personality and self-identity. Of great importance is the quality of relations with parents or caretakers, as is the influence of other intimate ties (family or otherwise) that have had an impact on the early formation of the individual psyche. Subsequent significant events, people and crises also leave their mark and are part of the overall trajectory of an individual's psychobiography. In this sense it traces out the critical points in the unfolding of their personal development.

Psychobiography supplies an account of the way in which a person has been uniquely constituted, emotionally. It tells us about the nature of their psychological resilience as it reflects their life experiences. In the context of the previous example, a psychobiography would supply us with clues about how the rejected lover would respond to their loss (of control). For instance, a history of consistent abandonment (by parents or friends) may have left the individual psychologically vulnerable and unable to bear the loss without serious emotional damage.

In contrast, the psychobiography may furnish us with a picture of a very secure individual, able to deal with such events with minimum mental disturbance. Thus the psychobiography gives an impression of the psychological constitution and emotional predisposition of any particular individual, and their likely reaction to disruptive life events and problems. In short it provides us with an estimate of their ability to deal with the changing circumstances of life.

Current Life Situation

While psychobiography is a summation of the evolutionary sweep of an individual's life span, by contrast the concept of 'current life situation' carries the story forward into the present. It is a representation of 'how things have turned out' or 'what they came to', expressed in terms of a 'frozen' point in time. But just as we can say that psychobiography provides clues to a person's self-mastery, the 'current life situation' may be understood as an object of control in its own right. In the same way that it is possible to talk of the extent (or lack) of control over self and over others, it is possible to speak of control over one's current life situation.

Current life situation is a more inclusive concept in the sense that it is the 'master' site of control which subsumes and embraces all the others. It is a summation of the overall state-of-play of control, as expressed in the totality of the person's current life circumstances. In this sense it is what I have elsewhere termed (Layder 1998) a 'bridging concept' anchored in both objective and subjective aspects of social reality. Objectively it refers to a moment in time in an ever-changing network of relationships that are socially tied to the individual and that have a significant influence over their lives. The network is 'objective' in the sense that it strays far beyond the focal individual and has an independent influence. It represents the balance of control between a person and the totality of their current relationships and circumstances.

Unlike other socially 'objective' concepts such as 'social class', 'social group' or 'lifestyle', 'current life situation' is unique to that individual. Each person's network is comprised of a different set of individuals with their own unique social circumstances. In this respect the concept is individualized in a way that other social concepts are not. Lifestyle, for example, only makes sense as an experience that can be socially shared by those wishing to adopt a similar lifestyle.

However, this network of relationships cuts across several distinct areas of an individual's (public and private) life. Thus the network includes different life (not 'lifestyle') sectors that have their own networks shearing off tangentially from the focal network. Thus there will be several sub-networks formed around work life, family relationships, friendships and so on. The degree of connectedness between the sectors (work, family, leisure) varies but its extent and quality depend on several factors, including the individual's decision to create or obstruct such links. One person may be happy with a high degree of integration and overlap between the sectors while others may rigorously defend the privacy of their family life or other intimate relationships and resent it if their work responsibilities 'force' them to establish closer connections between private and public spheres.

Such patterns of segmentation within networks mean that at any particular time, the individual may be 'in control' of one sector (reflected say, by success at work), while at the same time another sector may be raging 'out of control', as when a marriage is failing or undergoing a crisis. Conversely, a stable and satisfying private (emotional) life may be offset by problems at work (say a bullying boss or threatened redundancy). Of course each sub-sector will have its own small history and will tend to pull in different directions, making a variety of emotional demands on the individual at different times. But it is the network as a whole that reflects the degree and quality of control that the individual has over their current life situation.

Emotion, Control and Current Life Situation

The extent of an individual's control over their life situation bears a close relation to his or her state of mind and how well or badly they are getting on with the various members of their network. It hardly needs to be said that these emotional and experiential involvements crucially influence a person's sense of personal identity and emotional responses to their lives in general. Are they satisfied with their current situation, with what they have achieved and with the quality of their relationships? Does it represent a failure in some way? A failure to achieve, a sense of thwarted ambitions? Does it represent tolerable 'misery' in the face of the vagaries of fate? To what extent does the person feel in control of their relationships including work, friends, family?

The individual also has a wider view of life, which to a large degree is based on their response to more particular relationships. If they are not happy with their interpersonal relationships, there is a good chance that this will colour their broader emotional reaction to the world in general. This involves asking questions of the individual such as: Do they feel alienated, or unduly alone in the world? Do they feel comfortable with life? Are they able to deal with problems? Do they feel defeated by life and pessimistic about being able to change their circumstances? In all these respects, current life situation reflects the emotional tenor of an individual's response to their current circumstances.

A person's emotional response to their current life situation is directly linked to their feelings and sense of power. If they feel defeated by and pessimistic about life in general, they are also more likely to experience a sense of powerlessness. If an individual already feels relatively powerless, then their actual ability to improve their circumstances will be further undermined.

As the 'master' site that indicates a spread of personal control, 'current life situation' is multi-dimensional and reflects different (ontological) features of reality. Thus it is attendant to both objective and subjective features of social life. Objectively, it is a network of social relationships that play a significant role in the focal individual's life. But perhaps the more important characteristic of current life situation is an anchoring in the experience and viewpoint of the focal person. Without this subjective anchoring, its real significance as the locus of controlling influence in an individual's life is obscured.

Personal Control, Stress and Illness

It has been found that a loss or lack of personal control at work can place an individual under so much stress that it may eventuate in physical illness such as coronary heart disease or hypertension (Steptoe and Appels 1991; Syme 1991). It is also documented that illnesses of a psychosomatic nature such as chronic fatigue syndrome, anorexia and bulimia are stress related, although they are not exclusively associated with lack of personal control at work.

Cooper (1998) has suggested that the feeling of being out of control is probably the most significant factor in experiencing stress. He points to the rapidly changing organization of work in society in which the proliferation of short-term work contracts, as well as part-time and freelance work make for job insecurity while increasing workloads through demands for greater efficiency and productivity contribute to a stressful work environment. Being bullied by a boss or failing to convince immediate superiors that you are over-burdened and need help are also pressure-inducing. Stress caused either by work difficulties or other factors such as the break-up of a marriage or partnerships can result in the loss of a sense of humour, aggressiveness, the acquisition of lots of minor illnesses (often symptoms of chronic fatigue syndrome, see Fox 1996). Other 'wrong turnings', as Cooper describes them, include workaholism, drugs and alcohol.

Depression and Powerlessness

Gilbert (1992) has identified a number of elements of powerlessness that have an important influence on the experience of depression. A sense of defeat associated with the failure to achieve valued goals and objectives (such as getting a good job, having a successful marriage or being promoted) is often a cause of depression. Being ashamed or feeling inferior are emotions that typically accompany such failures – even though the goals may have been unrealistic in the first place, or may have been set for us by others, such as our parents.

Powerlessness in relationships is also a precipitating factor – as when a person is dominated, put down or abused by another, leading to feelings of worthlessness and self-blame. These are similar to features of emotional terrorism and domestic (women) abuse. Gilbert suggests that a consequence of submissiveness and compliance of a person who is thus dominated, is that their self-development is thwarted. Another kind of powerlessness is the inability to escape from a relationship or a particular situation because of fear and guilt about leaving.

For example, escaping from an unsatisfying marriage may be made difficult for some because of worries about what will happen if they do leave. People who are unhappy at work may fear that if they leave they will be unable to find another job. Over-dependence on relationships or situations like this, and the fear and guilt they produce, can develop into a chronic lack of assertiveness. Finally, powerlessness may be experienced as an inability to attract others. In this sense the individual feels they have no inner power and confidence to make others value them – to see them as talented, beautiful or able. Instead, they see themselves as unattractive, boring and worthless and this leads inevitably to a sense of failure and shame.

As Gilbert points out, 'in all these there is a loss of control over one's desires, destiny and lifestyle' (1992: 472). However, a sense of belonging is also important and this interacts with other features of power and control. A sense of belonging has to do with a person's feeling and valuing that they are a part of a relationship, a group or a network. A lack of control in various areas – those I have previously referred to as life sectors – may feed into, or undermine, a sense of belongingness.

For instance, a depressed person often feels cut off from others and believes that others do not or cannot understand them. This may contribute to a strong sense of being an outsider, rejected by others. Also the feeling of not having value – not playing a useful role in relationships or that others do not appreciate them, is common in depression. Sometimes a person will have such a meagre sense of self-value that they eventually perceive themselves as a burden to others and may even contemplate suicide.

Loss of Meaning, Uncertainty and Control

Much of an emotional nature is tied up and invested in certain activities and relationships, and their loss may also be associated with a general loss of meaning in our lives, as Ernest Becker (1974) has argued. Thus a disabling accident, chronic illness or the end of a love affair may precipitate a general sense of meaningless and emptiness. This might also be accompanied by feelings of dread, anxiety, lack of joy, a sense of deadness and pointlessness.

In this respect the robustness of self-identity depends on the ability to control the current life situation and particular relationships within it. Pride and self-esteem are invested in being in control and dealing with things effectively. If you suddenly realize you cannot cope with some misfortune like the loss of a partner or stress at work, then it will have a major impact on your attitude to yourself and to your self-identity. A complicating factor may involve the attempt to cling on to the depressed self, rather than move towards a healthier, newly emergent self.

Partly this may be because embracing the old self has certain benefits, rewards or hidden pay-offs attached to it (such as not having to make an effort socially, or avoiding the pain and suffering entailed in attempting to combat sadness). Although the depressed self-identity may have been responsible for locking the person into misery and unhappiness, paradoxically, over time it might have established itself as a comfortable and reliable part of their lives. In addition, reluctance to change the self may be perceived as a major bulwark against doubt and uncertainty. As Lott observes, symptoms of depression are strongly related to basic human needs, particularly those concerned with 'the need for psychological self-defence, the need for a sense of personal significance, the need to maintain a sense of certainty no matter how high the cost' (1999: 25). He argues that uncertainty is the biggest fear we face as human beings, since the world itself is a deeply uncertain place that we can only grasp partially and fleetingly.

In order to come to terms with such a chaotic world, from our earliest childhood we create our own inner worlds to try to insulate ourselves against the outer uncertainty of arbitrary misfortunes that strike from time to time. We can either believe that the world is random and we have no hope of controlling its effects on us, or we can make sense of it in terms of our inner worlds and the beliefs that sustain it. If, for example, you believe that only bad things happen to bad people, then this may lead to depression, which, in turn may reconfirm your beliefs. Some people cling to their depression because it protects them from contemplating the idea that the world is truly random, chaotic and chronically uncertain.

Ontological Insecurity and Loss of Control

Depressive reactions to different kinds of powerlessness certainly involve some 'debilitation' of the individual, especially in terms of being able to handle aspects of social life. However, they are not usually associated with a complete crippling of action or the loss of grip on reality that is linked with more severe psychotic mental illness. Laing (1969) has pointed out that an erosion of ontological security, in particular, can have such debilitating effects including a loss of a general grip on reality and this is what happens in psychotic illnesses like schizophrenia.

Ontological insecurity is an extension and intensification of what could be termed 'normal insecurity', which is linked with mild social phobias, sensitivities, shyness, withdrawal and so on. We all experience these milder forms of insecurity, but the more intense variety takes the form of uncertainties and anxieties around personal value, worth, identity and relation to other people. In short, self-identity becomes very fragile while social relationships are experienced as threatening.

Such assaults on the self undermine confidence and reliance on personal resources, especially at times when the individual is vulnerable. The ability to be self-directional and to choose one's behavioural options becomes compromised. Such insecurity is particularly disabling when life becomes a constant struggle for basic self-survival and self-preservation. An intense and chronic lack of certainty around identity, personal efficacy and agency makes it very difficult for the individual to control and influence other people, since most of his or her energies are devoted to the struggle for self-preservation.

Their preoccupation with keeping themselves 'alive' in an existential sense means that it is only possible to exert 'negative' control or influence over others, such as keeping emotional distance or refusing to 'acknowledge' them. It can result in a exclusively 'inward' turn, linked with more or less complete social withdrawal (as in catatonic schizophrenia). However, another possibility is that problems in social relationships (being difficult to get on with, irritability, bitterness and so on) can result in a further, outwardly aggressive response towards others.

In this sense the inner failure is also directed outwards, and is likely to involve a progressive deterioration in social relationships. This is what typically happens in paranoia, in so far as the paranoid person gradually becomes excluded from relationships and groups to which he or she once belonged because of increasing problems in dealing with them (Lemert 1962). The individual's inability to stem the loss of power and control has a negatively spiralling effect which brings them further and further into conflict with others.

Serial Murder as a Response to Control Failure

It is appropriate here to take up once again some elements of previous discussions. Two questions in particular are pertinent. First, what is the relation between various kinds of 'over' or 'exploitative' control and mental disorder? Second, can some examples of obviously successful domination and manipulation also be considered as responses to failures to control? The discussion begins with the latter question first.

At the end of the previous chapter it was suggested that the motivations of serial murderers often reflect their responses to a lack of control, a failure of control, or felt powerlessness over themselves, others or their current life situations. Thus their arrogation of absolute control over others by murder is a way of dealing with these inner or personal weaknesses and their failure to make a mark on the world in any conventional or morally legitimate sense. There are a number of different but closely related aspects to this pattern of motivation.

Jeffrey Dahmer and Dennis Nilsen are good examples of the urge to kill as a desperate response to failure to make their lives work through benign control. For them, serial murder was a desperate attempt to make their lives work at all! They lacked self-identities that could provide them with reliable, effective and executive agency in everyday life. Consequently, they were unable to induce or otherwise influence others into their orbit, or to properly bond with them. Hence real intimacy was not possible. Nor could they persuade others to be interested in anything more than transient sexual encounters. They manifestly failed to create or maintain intimate relationships – the very stuff of basic human existence. In short, they were unable to make benign control work for them.

Because they lacked capacities to attract and bond with others that we 'normally' take for granted, they resorted to creating illusory and distorted intimacy by the most hideous and depraved means. Both Nilsen and Dahmer kept dead bodies, sometimes dismembered, often for weeks or months on end in order to hold on to, or possess 'loved' ones who would otherwise have 'abandoned' them immediately after a brief sexual encounter.

Other serial murderers appear to have a particular difficulty in dealing with rejection or perceived humiliation which is experienced acutely and intensely as a loss of power and control. While rejection is undoubtedly painful for anybody, it is normally dealt with as part of the routine uncertainties, misfortunes and disappointments of life. Ted Bundy is a case in point where rejection by a former fiancée impacted so heavily on his sensibility and self-esteem that it precipitated a murder spree as a way of trying to regain lost power and self-esteem.

Finally, many serial murderers strongly desire to be thought of as important or 'significant' and to shake off the feeling that they are 'nobodies' whose 'real' talents are overlooked by society. Both Bundy and Nilsen thought of themselves in this manner. Others, considering themselves as loners or outsiders, wish to achieve some kind of celebrity status or fame that has been consistently denied them (Ed Gein and Charles Manson fall into this category).

Domination, Crime and Control Failure

Similar arguments can be marshalled with regard to manipulative and exploitative control, which are less intense than serial murder but closely linked nevertheless with failures in personal control. As remarked in Chapter 5, emotional terrorism is often based on chronic insecurity or inferiority. A consequent hyper-sensitivity to criticism means that minor or trivial 'put-downs' or 'humiliations' are often blown out of all proportion and taken as direct threats to self-esteem, self-efficacy and competence. The use or threat of violence as an adjunct to emotional abuse (as in domestic violence) can be understood as an escalation and intensification of this kind of control. But in these cases exploitation and domination are responses to a failure either to deal with a weakness of the self or to resolve routine problems in a manner that embraces the mutuality of their partners or 'victims'. Problems of empathy and emotional intelligence are also at the forefront.

It is often supposed that in violent rape and serial murders, perpetrators lack totally the ability to empathize with others (Canter 1994). However, it is extremely rare for human beings to lack this ability completely. It is probably more accurate to say that the ability to empathize may be relatively 'undeveloped' in certain individuals, making it more difficult (and less likely) to use such skills reflexively on a regular basis. Evidence suggests that empathetic skills are present to at least some degree, but that perpetrators employ them selectively. That is, perpetrators may regard certain individuals (or types) as deserving empathy (say immediate family, relative and friends), while others (potential victims) are not. This was clearly the case with the serial murderer, Peter Sutcliffe (known as the Yorkshire Ripper), whose wife and close family regarded him as a very 'normal' husband and son (see Burn 1985), while he reserved his lack of empathic response specifically for prostitutes.

The same selective application of empathy in different areas of social life applies to a great many serial murderers. But the selectivity argument also appears to be relevant to cases in which the perpetrator switches between empathic and non-empathic reactions to the same individual (partners or victims) at different times. This is typical of emotional terrorists and abusers of women, who are at times 'charming', courteous and loving, but at other times violent, abusive and hateful. There is a problem here about distinguishing between real or genuine empathy and practised or artificial empathy designed to deceive and undermine the victim. But the very ability to simulate empathy suggests that the problem is not an absolute inability to empathize per se, but rather that the perpetrator actively chooses when, how and why empathy should be accorded to another.

In cases of emotional blackmail and other kinds of emotional manipulation, in order to be successful, the perpetrator needs to be able to recognize emotion in themselves and others. The ability to 'press the right buttons' – those that activate fear, guilt and vulnerability in victims – is essential. A crucial difference between this and 'similar' types of control is that the controller seeks psychological and emotional control of the victim rather than physical intimidation and domination. He or she wants to be able to manipulate chosen targets as 'emotional beings' by reaching into, and ruling, their inner psychic lives. It is an attempt to 'take over' victims' minds as the most effective way of influencing and controlling them. Whether this is ultimately more 'empathic' depends on how we understand and evaluate the suffering and hurt that is visited upon victims. A moral issue here concerns the extent to which the mental hurt of being manipulated is disabling and how this compares with physical suffering.

General criminal activities can be understood as responses to a perceived lack of control over individuals' lives. There are two variants. First, lack of success in education, work and so on breeds resentment, envy or disapproval of the apparent success of others. The second variant involves a straightforward rejection of the 'legitimacy' of conventional society and its material and status inequalities and thus, precipitates the 'simple' appropriation of status and material goods.

In most crimes that involve the appropriation of material goods, the victims and law enforcement agencies that stand in the way of perpetrators are viewed solely as obstacles to success. As such, there is no emotional tie between perpetrators and victims (except, of course, in exceptional cases where family or friends are targets). The targets of such crimes are not viewed as emotional beings with feelings, rights and interests that need to be taken into account. Empathy and other elements of benign control and influence are simply ignored in the 'rush to control' that characterizes criminal activities like theft, vandalism, fraud, armed robbery, gang violence and so on.

This is quite unlike the more extreme forms of violence, rape and murder, in which the victim 'represents' some imagined emotional bond, albeit inverted or hideously distorted, between the perpetrator and victim (and reflected in the perpetrator's feelings of humiliation, loss of self-esteem, powerlessness, loneliness, alienation and so on). It is also unlike those forms of emotional abuse and exploitation in which the victim is a focus of emotional interest to the perpetrator.

Even though emotional and physical terrorists are concerned to override the 'humanness' of their victims in the service of bringing them under absolute control, they are linked by a distorted notion of intimacy. Thus victims of this kind of abuse have something of 'a hold' over these kinds of perpetrator (something they want or desire) and hence there is a negative attraction or bond that keeps the abuser in thrall to the victim's absolute compliance and submission. This may account for the 'selectivity of empathy', referred to earlier, which typically characterizes the behaviour of such abusers.

Mental Disorder, Control Failure and Crime

In many kinds of neurotic (less severe) mental disorders like depression, there is a shying away from revenge-taking on others or regarding them as a 'cause' of misfortune. The response to a control loss or control failure is to turn inward and attack the self as inadequate, incompetent and not up to the challenges of life. In this sense a lack of efficacy feeds on itself. The more depressed the individual becomes, the more inclined they will be to withdraw from social life and shrink from its challenges. The more they blame themselves for this state of affairs, the more depressed and withdrawn they become in a self-perpetuating downward spiral. Control over others and life in general thus becomes increasingly difficult as attention and aggression are turned on the self. The same is true for some of the more serious mental disorders (like schizophrenia), in which a chronic insecurity around self-identity tends to close the individual off from social contact and which further undermines self-competence, confidence and the ability to influence and control others.

In these cases an individual's recovery depends on their ability to regain assertiveness and to control and influence others, benignly from a position of self-competence, agency and efficacy. The self-blame must somehow be transformed (possibly with the help of drugs or therapy) into a self-support system that acknowledges human frailty and vulnerability without being completely trapped, overwhelmed or rendered helpless by it. However, much depends on the individual's propensity for self-blame in the first place. Those who seek blame in others or external factors rather than themselves are more likely to come into conflict with others over control issues. In paranoid reactions for instance, the tendency to externalize blame for misfortune is progressively hardened when others resist by creating distance between themselves and the paranoid individual.

The idea of externalizing blame for perceived lack of power and control is a thematic element in both crime in general and some kinds of mental disorder, and it is therefore no real surprise that the combination of the two is a fairly potent mixture. Their effects collide explosively in the more extreme forms of crime that involve the need for the submission and absolute compliance of victims. Emotional (and/or physical) terrorists have strong elements of this combination, in that they try to alleviate and transform an inner weakness or failing by seeking to extirpate any control (benign or otherwise) that their victims may possess. However, their designs in this respect are limited by the fact that they are to some extent dependent on the continuance of the relationship and their psychological dependence on their victim-partners.

Serial murderers are able to go one step beyond this, because they have no 'real' relationship with their victims. They are 'strangers' chosen because they represent or symbolize some issue that impinges personally on the perpetrator (such as humiliation, lack of self-esteem or powerlessness). It is often the case that the issue of mental illness is raised in relation to such murderers, many of whom opt for an insanity plea as a means of legal defence. The legal proof of mental illness in such criminals often hinges upon their degree of awareness and responsibility for their actions.

Often the aim of their legal defence is to achieve a more 'lenient' sentence by claiming and proving 'diminished responsibility' at the time of the murders. But questions of awareness and responsibility are tangential to the fact that the behaviour of such individuals is characterized by a strongly forged conjunction between psychological weaknesses around control (over self, others and life situation) and a tendency to seek external 'solutions' (the murder of victims) as a means of alleviating, displacing or resolving internal psychological problems.

Conclusion: the Other Side of Control

No account of control would be complete without considering the implications of control loss for individual psychology and behaviour. In normal circumstances the experience of being in control, and its opposite of losing control, are closely allied and reflect the continually shifting balance of power in a relationship. However, if a 'normal' loss of control turns into a haemorrhage or becomes a permanent and serious deficit, then personal identity (and the resources that underpin it) will come under threat, possibly leading to illness. In malign forms of control, the duality of success and failure is even more accentuated. Usually in these cases, failures in self-control or an absence of social skills associated with 'normal' benign control, directly feed into a compulsion to exert coercive control over others.

Summary

- Success and failure in interpersonal control are closely intertwined in several different ways.
- How people deal with a loss of control is an important indicator of their psychological resilience, the stability of their personal identity, and their motivations towards others.
- An individual's psychobiography is a reliable source of clues as to their likely response to a failure in control. Also the level of control over current life situation is a sensitive barometer of a person's emotional state and behavioural predisposition.
- Stress, lack of personal control and feelings of powerlessness are strongly associated with certain physical and mental illnesses.
- More serious mental disorders are linked with ontological insecurity, uncertainty and massive failures in control.
- Although many serious crimes involve the 'successful' domination and control of others, they also reflect an anti-social response to control failure.
- There are strong associations between serial murder, mental disorder and control failure of various kinds.

7

Some Propositions about Human Behaviour

Preview

- Themes in social behaviour and interpersonal control as they are found in:

  - Everyday social encounters and relationships.
  - The problems posed by the individual's attempt to control his or her current life situation.
  - Loss of control and failures of control.

This chapter takes the form of a series of propositions about the nature of interpersonal control. The propositions are arranged into three sections, each of which concentrates on different issues about control.

Social Interaction and Interpersonal Control

1 The greater part of social life and human existence is lived in and through social relationships and social interaction. This requires us to participate in mutual 'management', influence and control to ensure that we all obtain 'something' (e.g. emotional satisfaction, reassurance) from each relationship, encounter or event. 'Normal' or 'healthy' control is based on *broadly equitable* transactions between two or more people, depending on the exact amount of power each individual possesses.

   If the transactions are radically unequal, then the control is no longer normal or healthy, it is pathological and exploitative. It becomes a fundamentally different kind of interpersonal power and control.

2 Normal, 'mutually benign' control is an essential and intrinsic feature of human behaviour and interpersonal interaction. Without it,

individuals would not be effective social agents capable of having an impact on their social environment.

In this respect *all social* behaviour is controlling, or is influenced by controlling impulses – from buying a train ticket, to inviting someone over for dinner, to falling in love. Interpersonal control, therefore, is not limited to a narrow band of unhealthy, competitive and exploitative relationships. All social behaviour is control. Control is what social behaviour is essentially about. However, there are different types and degrees of control ranging from mutual benign control (the normal type, intrinsic to human relationships) to pathological types that involve manipulation, exploitation and domination driven by excessive selfishness and an absence of empathy.

3   Mutual benign control is by far the most pervasive in human affairs. It is an 'achieved' kind of control that depends on enlisting the support and consent of others. It takes account of others' interests, wishes and needs and in this sense is genuinely 'mutual'. Benign control is essentially non-competitive in any serious or ruthless sense, although it may involve elements of playful competition (as in mickey-taking or jockeying for conversational space). It is not designed for the explicit purpose of 'getting the better' of someone else or putting them down in any way. It is achieved through persuasion, charm, tact, love, argument, 'gentle manipulation', seduction (social or sexual) or any other benign form of influence.

The various forms of malign or exploitative control, on the other hand, are not 'achieved' through mutual consent. They are simply 'taken' or 'stolen' and rely on taking advantage of others who have less power or are more vulnerable. They are appropriated (rather than achieved), through exploitative manipulation and are characterized by a lack of compassion and empathy for those who are victims. It is the controller's wishes, needs and interests that have priority and often are the exclusive basis of these kinds of control.

Exploitative control is based on deception, intimidation, threats and the manipulation of rewards and punishments. It may be employed in conjunction with physical violence or its threat. It may also operate as pure psychological terrorism and manipulation. Although in many respects mutual benign control is starkly different from malign control, it is important not to see it as morally pure. All behaviour is 'selfish' to varying degrees because we are creatures of mixed motives.

4   The necessity for control in human relationships centres around two kinds of existential problems. First there is the problem of obtaining emotional (and other kinds of psychological) satisfaction that only

other people can provide for us. In order to do this, we must attract others into our orbit of influence (and control). Ideally, benign control allows us to fulfil ourselves emotionally while also helping to do the same for others, in a reciprocal arrangement.

Second there are problems that centre on uncertainty in social interaction. Uncertainty is generated by unpredictability in individual behaviour. Although we may know somebody very well, we can never know him or her completely. They are always capable of surprising us. Also, situated activity is such that its 'outcome' is never certain or within the control of any one individual (that is, in non-coercive situations). Thus uncertainty of outcome is an intrinsic feature of encounters.

5   Individuals approach interaction with a controlling orientation and a predisposition to cope with uncertainty and the management of desires that arise during encounters. The orientation to control reflects an 'anticipatory readiness' to deal with such problems.

6   In its benign forms the enactment of control is a subtle and sensitive operation that often goes on below the surface awareness of the participants. As such, the operation and dynamics of mutual control are rarely explicitly discussed. What participants actually talk about in the form of 'topics of conversation' are the behavioural effects of various controlling stratagems.

Benign control is accomplished through a subtle and flexible accommodation to the matters and problems that arise during interaction. Exploitative varieties of control are employed in more insensitive, unsubtle and heavy-handed ways.

7   The attempt to 'accomplish' benign control is only ever partially realized; it is never fully finished. The search for control in one area – say, an attempt to persuade a friend to be more open emotionally – is simply displaced by a refocusing and an attempt at partial control in another area – say, trying to convince the friend that your advice about a specific matter serves their best interests. This is very different from exploitative forms of control in which the aim is to achieve as complete a hold over the other in as many areas as possible.

8   The aim of benign control is practical in the sense that it is an attempt to achieve an outcome (a changed state of affairs) – such as the renewal of a personal bond or the dissolution of a relationship. But the aim is also partly 'fiduciary', involving elements of trust between participants. An example of this would be the transition from friendship to sexual love – a move that requires more trust and intimacy.

9   In so far as the controlling impulse is related to the interactional problems of uncertainty and unpredictability, then personal control is also linked with the attempt to deal with existential anxiety, insecurity and doubt.

10 To an extent the controlling impulse is an attempt to create and recreate ontological security – a solid sense of oneself and one's lived reality. Wresting personal control is the active grappling with the inherent uncertainty of social interaction and routine threats to self-esteem and status.

 The enactment of routines does not necessarily create or sustain ontological security and certainly cannot guarantee it. In fact the ritualized enactment of routines is often indicative of a deadening of emotional and psychological responses (lack of aliveness). It signals 'dis-ease' with the self, pathology rather than 'ease' or health.

 The active, chronic search for (partial) benign control is crucially important in keeping insecurity at bay. It is an attempt to find small pockets of certainty, safety and predictability, and to create the comforting illusion that such small certainties exist in a chaotic and uncertain world. A person must convince her or himself that it is relatively safe to act, even though there are always elements of risk attached to any behaviour. The individual needs to be able to 'carry on' in encounters and 'carry through' with incipient acts.

 Ontological security is not a passive outcome of routine. It is an active ingredient of creatively controlling action, which, in turn, is a response to existential anxiety, uncertainty and doubt about interactional outcomes. Furthermore, ontological security is not a 'fixed quantum' possessed by individuals; rather it is continually, but only ever partially, achieved in and through social interaction. The degree of security varies in relation to different situations and circumstances as well as at different points in a person's psychobiography.

11 Benign control is not essentially concerned with competitiveness or stealing energy from others. It is about having a personal stake in, and commitment to, a future state of affairs. Stated differently, benign control is a person's attempt to fashion the future so that it accords as much as possible with their own and others' desires.

12 Effective personal control is the capacity to sustain a 'managed' projection of the self through interactional space and time. The 'managed' nature of the projection protects the integrity of the self by keeping anxiety at reasonable levels and maintaining its wholeness, realness, competence and efficacy.

13 The mutuality of benign control 'facilitates' social interaction, lending dynamism to encounters. In this sense such control does not set out to be control 'over', as it tends to be in domination or exploitation. Rather, it encourages genuine mutuality in interaction.

14 Of course, in all control relationships both parties have a certain amount of power and thus it has a reciprocal nature (even though in domination the exchanges are unequal). However, in the benign form there is no 'dialectic' at work (Giddens 1984). A dialectic implies incompatibility and conflict of interest. But benign control depends upon the sharing of aims and interests. It is mutual and reciprocal, but not dialectical. However, benign control is not about complete sharing of interests or aims. Mutual benign control is essentially about taking others' interest into account.

   Thus there is a continuum between having the best interests of someone in mind and simply being mindful that they *have* interests that must taken into account, if only minimally. Both are forms of benign control at different ends of the continuum. Although benign control is, therefore, not necessarily harmonious or conflict-free, it does require a broad compatibility of aims and interests.

15 Benign control sometimes involves an inherent asymmetry of power, but does not, thereby, rule out the possibility of mutual care and respect. Unequal power may generate mild or moderate conflicts of interest whilst the overall objectives remain broadly compatible and the atmosphere remains relatively harmonious.

   There are, for example, inherent inequalities of power in parent–child, or guardian/protector/carer relationships with vulnerable individuals (the mentally ill, disabled, aged, chronically ill). Generally the guardians, protectors or carers are more powerful than their charges, but the relationship is based on the assumption that they will act in the best interests of their charges. The obvious exceptions are, of course, those relationships in which abuse or exploitation of some kind is taking place. But if the relationship is working properly, that is benignly and mutually, there are two modes in which power and control may be conveyed.

   First there is what might be termed *open-ended or suggestive control*, in which the protector or carer merely offers 'advice' and leaves the final decision or outcome in the hands of the 'subject', who is free to 'resist' or reject the advice. In such a case the power holder will use phrases like; 'This might be best for you' or 'I think you would be more comfortable in sheltered accommodation', and so forth.

   Second, in *imperative or closed control* the subject has little or no choice in the matter. It is based on unilateral decisions purportedly taken in the best interests of the person. This is illustrated in the use of phrases like; 'Sorry but I'm doing this [calling the doctor, say] because it's best for you' or 'You must not open the door to anyone unless there is someone with you'.

16 Benign control is strongly linked with gift exchanges and 'offerings' involving material objects like money, property, drugs and so on, but also 'trust' offerings and exchanges like compliments, love, support, friendship, invitations to dinner and companionship. The most important of these are about psychological or emotional matters since these deeply affect mental well-being.

Gaining the approval or 'recognition' of others necessitates having something to offer them 'in return' (such as a talent for 'listening' or an ability to understand their problems). Deep-seated feelings such as that of 'acceptance' and being valued or loved for ourselves are equally important focal points of exchange in relationships. A strong and stable sense of security, self-confidence and self-esteem can only emerge if there is some mutually satisfying balance in gift exchanges.

17 Part of the impulse to control is fuelled by the attempt to avoid being at the mercy of life, of chance and fortune, of one's boss, other people and so on. In this sense it is a completely natural, almost 'instinctive' urge to survive in the social world and to pre-serve some autonomy and independence from others. 'Avoiding dependence' on other's is perhaps, more accurate since it is an attempt to be relatively free of others' demands and to preserve existing freedoms. The initial establishment of control is frequently difficult and accentuates the elusiveness that often characterizes the search for control. Realizing this, people cling on to whatever control they possess.

18 The controlling impulse is closely linked with the tension between separateness and relatedness (or independence and involvement in social life). Although an ability to be independent is essential for life in the modern world, there is constant pressure to be part of the crowd and to join in with others. This dilemma cannot be resolved in any final sense because a shift or tilt in one direction directly threat-ens the other side of the dilemma. A display of independence is a potential 'threat' to involvement with others, while over-dependence compromises separateness and autonomy.

Social entanglements open up the possibility of being controlled by others and may prompt resistance or countervailing control games. Conversely, being unduly alone or 'separate' poses a threat to security and self-identity. We need others to confirm our social connectedness and the 'reality' of personal existence and individuality. This dilemma directly affects how insecure or anxious we become in our daily lives and influences our dealings with others.

Control and Current Life Situation

19 Human beings try to achieve a natural balance of control in and over their relationships, interactions and lives in general. The more an individual feels 'in control' of these areas, the more they experience life as comfortably 'manageable'. This sense of mastery and efficacy generates the conviction that life is fulfilling and worthwhile. Possessing a balance of control and of being able to affect one's circumstances leads to feelings of satisfaction, happiness, security, pride and euphoria.

Conversely, a lack of balance creates a sense that one's life and relationships are 'out of control' and unmanageable. This, in turn, produces feelings of helplessness, insecurity, anxiety and unease. It is necessary to feel to some extent 'in control' of your life to remain mentally healthy and to sustain a 'normal' social life.

20 A 'balance' of control over current life situation is never definitive, perfect or complete because:

(a) There is always an uneven spread of control between different life sectors (marriage/partnership, work/career (unemployment), self, friendships and leisure activities) at any one time.

(b) The amount of personal control within particular sectors (say partnership or career) at different times is fluid – it constantly shifts and alters.

(c) There is variation in the balance of control according to different points of reference: over an individual lifetime (psychobiography), within particular situations, or in terms of locations, settings or contexts.

21 Relationships will only endure as long as the reciprocity in them is broadly equitable and mutually satisfying. If this balance alters leading to dissatisfaction in one of the partners, then there are several alternative possibilities.

(a) The dissatisfied partner may try to restore the previous 'balance' while the substance of the exchanges may alter in the process.

(b) He or she may learn or decide to accept a 'new balance' after negotiation and consultation in which their dissatisfactions are, at least nominally, taken into account.

(c) They may accept reduced control and less satisfaction and acquiesce to the other's increased control.

(d) They may seek to terminate or leave the relationship. In certain cases this may be very difficult. Individuals may become trapped in unsatisfactory relationships by physical intimidation, guilt, emotional blackmail, economic or emotional dependence and so on.

Over-control and Failures of Control

22 A healthy response to a real or threatened loss of control would be to effectively counteract it when it occurs. However, people have differing levels of sensitivity and tolerance and sometimes find it difficult to determine what constitutes a satisfactory balance. Some are prone to misjudgement in this respect. They may obsess about losing control even before it has occurred or they may be deluded about others trying to control them. As a reaction to an 'imagined' threat, an individual may ratchet up their level of control even before there has been any weakening of their own power base. This kind of over-control creates maximum discomfort for all concerned. There are several forms:

(a) *The 'control freak'* displays an unhealthy concern with being in command or wanting to be in control of everything and everyone around them. Such control may take a broad range of forms. In the work world it may manifest itself as an unwillingness or inability to 'delegate' because of a basic belief – sometimes warranted and sometimes unfounded – that others are not capable of doing a good enough job. In the domestic or family sphere, a control freak may try to arrange and organize each and every aspect of others' lives.

The control freak may use seriously unhealthy control such as emotional blackmail or terrorism (see below). However, generally speaking, the control freak's problems are fundamentally neurotic in character and hence represent the more benign side of over-control. For those exposed to it, the control freak's behaviour is generally regarded as 'interference', or as indicating a 'lack of confidence' or lack of 'belief' in others' abilities. Although these are often 'undermining', they do not pose the same level of threat to others as other kinds of over-control.

(b) *Co-dependence or 'addictive love'* involves mutual over-control. It exists when two people are excessively dependent on each other (for psychological support, company, self-esteem, and so on), and as a result, restrict each other's personal growth and independence. Characteristically such lovers have a need to control each other's behaviour and exclude others so that the psychological support gained from their symbiosis is not dissipated or undermined.

(c) *Emotional blackmail* is achieved either in a passive, behind-the-scenes manner, or from rather blunt or even confrontational means. In either case, blackmailers use intimate knowledge of the vulnerabilities and personal 'secrets' of those who are the targets of the blackmail to obtain their compliance. They threaten to withhold love or approval, or to reveal intimate secrets unless the victim does what the blackmailer wants.

(d) *Emotional or psychological terrorism* relies more overtly on bullying and open manipulation to achieve its effects. The tactics used may range from sheer intimidation and angry outbursts to the use of prolonged silences (and other forms of psychological cruelty). These 'punishments' are a crude way of controlling relationships since they do not rely (as they often do in emotional blackmail) on the more subtle manipulation of feelings. However, it is possible to find emotional blackmail shading into terrorism and vice versa. A terrorist is compelled to control in this manner because of chronic insecurity, lack of confidence or self-esteem. But instead of turning inwards and engaging in self-punishment or self-hate, the moodiness is turned outwards towards others.

(e) *Domination* is an extreme form of over-control in which an individual or a group attempts to exploit and manipulate others for their own ends. Domination is a broad-ranging category. It may refer to the power and control of groups (like social classes, political parties, terrorist organizations and so on) over other groups or populations. At the other extreme it may indicate an individual's attempt to manipulate another (such as a partner, friend or relative) or even a small group of such people. Of course, particular individuals may be part of some larger collectivity within which they wield personal or charismatic power (for example, Hitler in Nazi Germany).

Domination by individuals over other individuals is a typical feature of everyday encounters. It features in 'friendships', marriages and work relationships. Domination may be linked with other types of over-control (such as co-dependence or emotional terrorism). Pure domination, however, is the assertion of power and control without justification or contextual motive that may serve to explain or rationalise it.

In summary, over-control is typically about establishing control over others in order to orchestrate their behaviour and tie it in with the controller's interests and objectives. A fear of, or preoccupation with, the possibility of a loss of control often leads to attempts to pre-empt it before it occurs. This usually takes the form of a continuous increase in intensity and spread of control.

23 By contrast, a lack or a chronic loss of personal control produces a move 'out of balance' in the opposite direction of over-control. An

individual's lack of control over her or his job or relationships is often associated with physical and mental pressure. Tension, stress, anxiety and irritability may be preludes to disorders that have both physical and mental correlates, including hypertension, strokes, depression, alcoholism and workaholism.

A spiralling and concerted loss of control (over several life sectors) is associated with a deteriorating mental state and an increasing inability to sustain a 'normal' social life. Neurotic responses to such circumstances include the milder forms of mental illness such as anxiety or existential neuroses, depression and personality disorders. They also include such illnesses as chronic fatigue syndrome (ME), anorexia and bulimia that may become entrenched and severe in their consequences.

Despite the troubling feelings that attend such disorders – meaninglessness, fatigue, fear and anxiety – sufferers remain in touch with reality and retain some grip on self-identity (although this varies). While they retain this basic anchor in the real world, they have at least some control over their lives and what happens to them. They may even seek help (therapy, counselling, medical advice and so on), in an effort to counteract the illness. Confusion and anxiety about how to deal with the control loss are common and may lead to a sense of helplessness and despair. Whatever is the case, sufferers are constantly engaged in a battle to cling on to, or claw back, some control.

More severe psychotic responses include manic depression, paranoia, schizophrenia, schizoid conditions and suicidal feelings. These are associated not only with a chronic lack of control over life circumstances (current life situation), but also with distorted perceptions of self and reality. Typically sufferers are out of touch or out of synch with reality and experience identity confusion. The most extreme form of this is where sufferers find themselves in an 'intolerable' situation in which all routes back to health – the recovery of control of their lives and feelings – seem to be permanently blocked. The individual perceives no alternatives and the possibility of recovering lost control appears futile. The most extreme example of this is suicide, in which taking one's life is seen as the only solution to 'impossible pressures' that have built up and produced a situation that is desperately out of control.

24 Crime and violence can be understood as pathological forms of control. In this sense simply taking, stealing or appropriating control (over people and material resources) is a response to a perceived deficit or inequity. Crime is a short-cut to control that would, through legitimate routes, require much greater investments of time, skills and energy. The 'advantage' of crime and violence is that a perceived

control imbalance may be restored simply by a seizure or arrogation of other people's money, property or status.

Much crime and violence are linked with the appropriation of material goods (and what they denote in terms of social status). However, the emotional aspects of crime such as excitement, risk, anger, humiliation, revenge and so on play an important role in the drama of control, as do issues of identity, self-esteem, security, deception and psychological manipulation. Deep emotional and psychological issues (such as lack of empathy and depersonalization of victims) are particularly relevant in cases involving extreme violence like serial murder.

Summary

- All social behaviour involves significant elements of interpersonal control that provide a necessary and dynamic feature of social life.
- Although largely overlooked, benign control is ubiquitous and pervasive in social life.
- Effective control reduces uncertainty and anxiety and buttresses security and personal identity. It adds to a sense of efficacy and competence in social interaction.
- Control over an individual's current life situation can never be perfectly realized because of variations in relation to different sectors. However, it strongly influences the quality of a person's emotional experience and sense of well-being.
- On the one hand, failures in control are associated with manipulative and malign behaviour, and on the other, they are also linked with problems around personal identity and mental health.

8

The Lost Heart: Theory & Research

Preview

- Social research and theory development: implications of the analysis of interpersonal control.
- Problems with current approaches to theory and research.
- The adaptive approach and cumulative knowledge.

Since the propositions about human behaviour presented in the previous chapter serve to bring together many of the specific themes of the book as a whole, I shall use this final chapter to reflect on some more general issues. The specific manner in which I have analysed interpersonal control has implications for the links between theory and social research. More particularly, the foregoing analysis highlights the productive link that may exist between general social theory and theory-generating social research. In this chapter I shall examine what has so far remained implicit about these themes.

Interpersonal Control: Theory and Research

The example of general theory that has figured most has been that of my own 'theory of social domains' (or 'domain theory'). Initially this was put to use to show how the agency-structure problem in social theory links up with the study of interpersonal control. It was then used as a 'formative' (rather than a mere 'passive') backdrop for more focused theoretical analysis of the psychology of control and interpersonal encounters (Chapters 2 and 3). In Chapters 4–6 the theory of social domains was used as a resource in devising a formalised theory that outlined a typological model of interpersonal control across a wide range of substantive phenomena and areas of research. Finally, Chapter 7 outlined some behavioural propositions themed around personal control. Although not explicitly part of the presentation, these propositions bear an organic relation to domain theory. Following this sequencing then, the use of domain theory shifted from a general theoretical role in Chapters 1, 2 and 3, to a less clear cut position in Chapters 4–7 in which questions of theory, data analysis and research were intermixed.

Let us examine this latter 'shift' in more detail. In Chapters 4–6 I used existing research on particular areas in which interpersonal control played a predominant role. This included a diverse range of topics from friendship and sexual intimacy at one extreme, to women abuse and serial murder at the other. The aim was to generate theory by bringing together a number of originally discrete pieces of research. In this sense the theory of domains did not simply dictate the terms of the theory of interpersonal control as it appears in these chapters. Rather, the theory of interpersonal control emerged from the interplay between three analytic strands:

1   The comparative analysis of different substantive areas (for example, intimacy in sexual relationships, emotional blackmail).
2   The analysis of research data in terms of theory deriving from the psychology of personal and interpersonal control.
3   The sifting and blending of theory in 2, with the relevant elements of the theory of social domains (particularly as it represents agency–structure linkages).

The resulting theory of interpersonal control that emerged from this interplay is an example of what I have elsewhere referred to as 'adaptive theory' (Layder 1998). That is the theory is neither 'given' through the simple application of prior theory (of whatever level of generality), nor is it given or informed simply by the data of research. Instead the theory adapts responsively to the findings of research while they, in turn, are subject to the scrutiny of (different levels of) theoretical filtration. Before unpacking these statements in more detail let me highlight the distinctiveness of this approach by comparing it with others.

Focused, In-depth Research

In the introduction I suggested that research on interpersonal control had emphasized the importance of depth of analysis in particular substantive areas such as family conversations, or domestic violence/women abuse. While 'depth' may, indeed, be an important aspect of research, it also limits the possibility of making general statements about interpersonal control.

First, depth analysis ensures knowledge of the particular area of research but does not touch on common features across a range of areas. By concentrating so fixedly on a particular substantive area, depth analysis deflects attention away from comparison with examples drawn from different, as well as similar, areas. This enables the researcher to develop ideas, concepts and empirical indicators in relation to that area (Glaser and Strauss 1967).

Second, because depth analysis is primarily focused on internal matters it is insulated from wider issues. It is thus prevented from connecting with different kinds of theoretical enterprise of the kind I shall discuss below. In-depth analysis adds to the stock of research information by producing relatively isolated 'islands' of knowledge. This slows down the development of genuinely cumulative knowledge that requires interchange and dialogue between areas of knowledge.

Grounded Theory

Grounded theory was developed as a move away from the idea of research as simply, or primarily, an empirical information gathering exercise. In it, research is concerned with generating (or building) theory from the data uncovered by research. By insisting that theory must be grounded and should only be developed through data collection and analysis, Glaser and Strauss (1967) argued that it was more secure and valid than other kinds of theory.

They were also critical of what they call 'speculative' theories, which they claim are not grounded in data. These theories are either the result of pure 'armchair theorising' or of research that has theory testing as its main purpose. In the first approach the theorist 'dreams up' a theoretical scheme that appears elegant and systematic but which, in reality, is arbitrary and speculative in that it bears no connection with the actual facts of the matter. Data is then forced to fit the theory that is then 'claimed' to explain the data.

Theory testing research starts out with a hypothetical explanation of some phenomenon; say suicide, or crime, and then gathers data in order to test out whether or not it is correct. Although this is less speculative than armchair theorising it is only marginally so, since it starts out from a prior hypothesis that is not grounded in data. Furthermore, the over-riding emphasis on 'testing out' prior hypotheses or concepts similarly tends to make the data fit the theory rather than the other way around.

Although the grounded theory approach has a point as compared with in-depth data-gathering approaches and has underlined the importance of theory construction, its view of theory is unnecessarily limited and arbitrarily restricts the possibilities of theory production in the accumulation of knowledge. The problem is its insistence that all theory must be ultimately derived from the analysis of the empirical data of research.

Initially this will be what Glaser and Strauss term 'substantive theory' – about a particular substantive area such as nursing or teaching. This may eventually take on a more formal, abstract and general form, after the accumulation of more evidence.

But this excludes general theory (such as the theory of social domains) or theories based on some prior hypothesis or that have theory testing as their main aim. To overcome these arbitrary restrictions we must make room for research that draws on general theory in an organic manner and which enhances theory-generating potential. To do this we must acknowledge that general theories, like the theory of social domains, represent different levels of empirical anchorage and are subject to more inclusive forms of evidential proof and validation. Furthermore, we must acknowledge that they refer to both objective and subjective aspects of social reality (rather than exclusively inter-subjective phenomena) and that they allow for the full complexity of theory data/indicator relationships.

General Theory

The theory of domains has been used in an organic manner by linking with a more specific theory of interpersonal control and different levels of data analysis and behavioural propositions. But it is rare for general theories to be used in such a manner. General theory too, tends to be inward looking – towards other theoretical matters. In this sense general theory and social research often seem isolated from each other without much in the way of real communication between them. Whatever attempts at connection there are, usually come from social researchers reaching out to social theory to help them conceptualize research data or to provide a 'theoretical framework' for it. Social theorists, however, sporadically refer to this or that study in order to buttress their own theoretical assumptions. Neither of these 'attempts' at interchange is particularly productive.

Sometimes whole (general) theoretical frameworks such as some variant of Marxist theory, or structuration theory, or developmental theory are used as a way of imposing some sense on the data. But this often entails forcing data into preconceived concepts and does nothing to advance knowledge. It merely reaffirms existing assumptions. Similarly, using particular concepts (from general theories) to 'spice up' or decorate research findings often simply adds a meaningless gloss or wrenches specific concepts out of a wider and more meaningful context.

General theories usually communicate with each other as a clash or confrontation of ideas and very rarely as a productive interchange involving empirical evidence. For the wider advancement of knowledge general theory must seek out organic connections with primary data-gathering projects that are concerned with theory generation. The method I have adopted in this present work is one way towards such an objective.

Theory-testing Research

As with grounded theory, theory-testing research (often associated with Merton) must be understood as a strategy and resource that may be drawn upon for specific purposes. In the approach adopted here, general theory (in this case domain theory) is not a framework against which evidence can be tested in a simple, straightforward manner. It is, rather, suggestive of ideas, concepts and hypotheses that might then be assimilated into a more specific theory of interpersonal control. Emerging ideas and concepts are evaluated against data or evidence as they are found in the resources being examined. But since the primary aim is to produce innovative theory, theory-testing elements should never become dominant, otherwise they will override and subvert this aim.

How Does This Apply To the Analysis of Interpersonal Control?

Rather than dictating more specific theory, the general theory in question is in the service of helping to generate lower level theoretical propositions. Thus general theory works in conjunction with emergent theory. The interchanges between the two are flexible and mutually supportive with the general theory providing guides, insights themes and so on, while the more specific emergent level applies brakes and checks, as well as alternative conceptualisations. Finally, the emergent theory generates behavioural propositions that are testable in the rather more traditional sense.

General Theory	The Theory of Social Domains
Specific, Emergent Theory	A Theory of Interpersonal Control
Elements of Above Theory	A Classification of Types of Control, Strategies of Control, Settings, Emotions, Relations between these Variables & Empirical Examples
Behavioural Propositions	24 Propositions about the nature of Interpersonal control: its psychological effects on individuals, their interactions, relationships and life situations.

The theory of domains did not directly suggest the classification of types and strategies of control and so on, but provided a means of reflecting on the causal relations and influences between different features of social reality (power and control and the domains of pychobiography, situated activity, social settings and contextual resources). By moving back and forth between these general ideas and particular examples of interpersonal control, it was possible to construct the classification of types and strategies of control and connect them with typical settings and forms of emotion. From here it was but a short step to deriving behavioural propositions about interpersonal control. Some of these resulted from 'thinking through' the implications of the emergent theory while others more directly reflect the underpinning data.

In both cases the behavioural propositions were, in a particular sense, 'derived' from the more general and abstract levels of theorising. 'Derived' in this sense does not mean simply 'deduced from' (as in the classical hypothesis-testing mode). The lower level (less abstract, more concrete), derivations were part of an ordered process of abduction – moving back and forth between the imaginative flow of theoretical ideas and the checks and balances imposed by data gathering and analysis.

This particular example of adaptive theorising shows that general theory can help in the formulation of concrete propositions about human behaviour of the kind presented in Chapter 7. It also emphasizes two other points. First, the important need for empirical (primary, data-gathering) research to concern itself with the formal implications of theory and the theoretical analysis of data. Second, it stresses the complementary need for general theory to concern itself more with tracing out its implications at the level of human behaviour in a very concrete manner.

But overall, theory should never simply be a decorous 'added extra' to the findings of research. It is only through theory development that empirical knowledge can be expressed in a generalised form. Only when knowledge is expressed in such a form can interconnections be discovered between diverse data sets and hitherto unrelated elements of theory – both general and specific. In short, the way to genuinely cumulative social scientific knowledge is to make theory generation more flexible, inclusive and sophisticated.

Summary

- The theory of social domains was drawn on to help develop an 'adaptive' theory of interpersonal control. In this approach theory adapts responsively to the findings of research while the data is subject to theoretical scrutiny.
- In-depth research, grounded theory and theory-testing research tend to either limit, or prohibit the role of general theory in research, while the use of general theory often bears little real relation to research findings.
- General theory (like the theory of social domains) can and should be used more frequently in social research to aid the development of behavioural propositions that are theoretically informed while also firmly anchored in research data.

References

Barbalet, J. (2001) *Emotion, Social Theory and Social Structure*. Cambridge: Cambridge University Press.

Becker, E. (1974) *Revolution in Psychiatry*. New York: Free Press.

Bernstein, B. (1973) *Class, Codes and Control*. Vol. 1. London: Paladin.

Blumer, H. (1969) *Symbolic Interactionism*. Englewood Cliffs, NJ: Prentice-Hall.

Bourdieu, P. (1977) *Outline of a Theory of Practice*. Cambridge: Cambridge University Press.

Branden, N. (1985) *Honouring the Self*. Los Angles: J.P. Tarcher.

Burn, G. (1985) *Somebody's Husband, Somebody's Son*. London: HarperCollins.

Canter, D. (1994) *Criminal Shadows*. London: HarperCollins.

Collins, R. (1983) 'Micromethods as a basis for Macrosociology', *Urban Life*, 12: 184–202.

Cooper, C. (1998) *Stop the World: Finding a Way through the Pressures of Life*. London: Hodder & Stoughton.

Craib, I. (1994) *The Importance of Disappointment*. London: Routledge.

Edwards, R. (1979) *Contested Terrain*. London: Heinemann.

Elias, N. (1978) *What is Sociology?* London: Hutchinson.

Forward, S. and Fraser, D. (1998) *Emotional Blackmail*. London: Bantam.

Foucault, M. (1980) *Power/Knowledge*. Brighton: Harvester Press.

Fox, J. (1996) *Surviving ME*. London: Vermillion.

Fromm, E. (1971) *The Art of Loving*. London: Allen & Unwin.

Garfinkel, H. (1967) *Studies in Ethnomethodology*. Englewood Cliffs, NJ: Prentice-Hall.

Giddens, A. (1984) *The Constitution of Society*. Cambridge: Polity.

Giddens, A. (1987) *Social Theory and Modern Sociology*. Stanford: Stanford University Press.

Giddens, A. (1991) *Modernity and Self-Identity*. Cambridge: Polity.

Gilbert, P. (1992) *Depression: The Evolution of Powerlessness*. Hove: Lawrence Erlbaum.

Glaser, B. and Strauss, A. (1967) *The Discovery of Grounded Theory*. Chicago: Aldine.

Goffman, E. (1967) *Interaction Ritual*. New York: Anchor.

Goffman, E. (1983) 'The interaction order', *American Sociological Review*, 48: 1–17.

Goleman, D. (1996) *Emotional Intelligence*. London: Bloomsbury.

Habermas, J. (1984) *The Theory of Communicative Action*. Vol. 1. Cambridge: Polity.

Habermas, J. (1987) *The Theory of Communicative Action*. Vol. 2. Cambridge: Polity.

Hale, R. (1998) 'The application of learning theory to serial murder', in R. Holmes and S. Holmes (eds) *Contemporary Perspectives on Serial Murder*. Thousand Oaks, CA: Sage.

Hochschild, A. (1983) *The Managed Heart*. Berkeley CA: University of California Press.

Holmes, R. and Deburger, J. (1998) 'Inside the mind of the serial murderer', in R. Holmes and S. Holmes (eds) *Contemporary Perspectives in Serial Murder*. Thousand Oaks, CA: Sage.

Horley, S. (2000) *The Charm Syndrome*. London: Refuge.

Jamieson, L. (1998) *Intimacy*. Cambridge: Polity.

Katz, J. (1988) *Seductions of Crime*. New York: Basic Books.

Kemper, T. (1978) *A Social Interactional Theory of Emotions*. New York: Wiley.

Laing, R. (1969) *The Divided Self*. Harmondsworth: Penguin.

Layder, D. (1993) *New Strategies in Social Research*. Cambridge: Polity.

Layder, D. (1997) *Modern Social Theory: Key Debates and New Directions*. London: University College London Press.

Layder, D. (1998) *Sociological Practice*. London: Sage.

Layder, D. (2005) *Understanding Social Theory*. Second edition. London: Sage.

Lemert, E. (1962) 'Paranoia and the dynamics of exclusion', *Sociometry*, 25: 2–20.

Lott, T. (1999) 'Story of the Blues', *Observer Magazine*, 21 Feb.

Malone, M. (1997) *Worlds of Talk*. Cambridge: Polity.

Manning, P. (1992) *Erving Goffman and Modern Sociology*. Cambridge: Polity.

Masters, B. (1993) *The Shrine of Jeffrey Dahmer*. London: Coronet.

Masters, B. (1995) *Killing for Company*. London: Arrow.

Mead, G. (1967) *Mind, Self and Society*. Chicago: Chicago University Press.

Peele, S. and Brodsky, A. (1974) *Love and Addiction*. London: Abacus.

Person, E. (1990) *Love and Fateful Encounters*. London: Bloomsbury.

Peters, T. and Waterman, H. (1995) *In Search of Excellence*. London: HarperCollins.

Piaget, J. (1952) *The Origins of Intelligence in Children*. New York: W.W. Norton.

Popper, K. (1972) *Objective Knowledge*. Oxford: Oxford University Press.

Rawls, A. (1987) 'The interaction order sui generis: Goffman's contribution to social theory', *Sociological Theory*, 5: 136–49.

Redfield, J. and Adrienne, C. (1995) *The Celestine Prophecy: An experiential guide*. London: Bantam.

Roy, D. (1973) 'Banana Time: job satisfaction and informal intereaction', in G. Salaman and G. Thompson (eds) *People and Organisations*. London: Longman.

Sartre, J-P. (1966) *Being and Nothingness*. London: Methuen.

Scheff, T. (1990) *Microsociology*. Chicago: Chicago University Press.

Steptoe, A. and Appels, A. (1991) *Stress, Personal Control and Health*. Chichester: Wiley.

Stewart, S. (1998) *Shattered Dreams*. London: Mainstream.

Stryker, S. (1981) *Symbolic Interactionism: a social structural version*. Englewood Cliffs, NJ: Prentice-Hall.

Swift, R. (1994) *Women's Pleasure*. London: Pan Books.

Syme, L. (1991) 'Control and health: a personal perspective', in A. Steptoe and A. Appels (eds) *Stress, Personal Control and Health*. Chichester: Wiley.

Tannen, D. (1987) *That's Not What I Meant*. London: Dent.

Tannen, D. (1992) *You Just Don't Understand*. London: Virago.

Tannen, D. (2002) *I Only Say This because I Love You*. London: Virago.

Turner, R. (1962) 'Role-taking; process versus conformity', in A. Rose (ed.) *Human Behaviour and Social Processes*. Boston: Houghton Mifflin.

Vaitkus, S. (1991) *How is Society Possible*. Dordrecht: Kluwer Academic.

Weber, M. (1964) *The Theory of Social and Economic Behaviour*. New York: Free Press.

Weinstein, E. and Deutschberger, P. (1963) 'Some dimensions of altercasting', *Sociometry*, 26: 454–66.

Winnicott, D. (1963) *Maturational Process and the Facilitating Environment*. London: Hogarth Press.

Index

abuse
  emotional 76–7
  women 83
adaptive theory 116, 120
addictive love 77–8, 111
agency
  emotion 12–13
  interpersonal control 13–14
  self as executive centre 26–7
  situated activity 11–12
  social 9–10
agency–structure
  attempts to resolve problem 3, 8–9
  institutional and interaction
      orders 19–20
altercasting 51–2
altruism 62
anti-social behaviour 29
anxiety
  controlling impulse 107
  insecurity 40–3
  uncertainty 38–40
appeals, personal and positional 31–2
assertiveness 70–1
attractors 52–3
authority 61, 62–3, 82
awareness 24–5

babies 28
balance of control 90, 110
behaviour
  appropriate 19
  mixed-motive 62
  propositions 104–14, 120
  social domains 48–9
  social settings 14, 47
  unintended impact on others 12
benign control
  agency 13
  balance of power 90
  control strategies 51–6
  essential feature of human
      behaviour 104–9

benign control *cont.*
  gift exchanges 109
  hiddenness 106
  incompleteness of attempts at
      106, 107
  intimacy 66–71
  introduction 1–2
  part of spectrum of control
      59–63, 87–8
  pathological control based on 76
  personal mastery 29
  serial murder 85–6
blackmail, emotional 29, 57,
      79–81, 111
blame 101–2
bullying 78–9
Burrell, Paul 72–3

careers 75–6
celebrity, negative 33–4
charm 53, 54, 83
children
  development 28–9
  ontological security 41
closed control 108–9
co-dependence 77–8, 111
coercion 57–8, 60, 61, 64
complicity 54–5
conceptual singularities 8–9
conformity 15
constructionism, social 36
contextual resources 48, 50
control
  see also individual types
  failures 89–103
  psycho-social development 27–9
  strategies 51–8, 61
  types and dimensions 59–65
control dramas 57
control freaks 111
controlling impulse 106–7
conversations 51–2
creativity 15, 17–18

crime
  externalization of blame 102
  loss of control 100–1
  as short-cut to control 84, 113
current life situation 13–14, 92–4, 110
customer management 55, 74

Dahmer, Jeffrey 86–7, 98–9
decision-making 25, 27
depression 91, 95–7, 101–2, 112–13
development, childhood 28–9
dialectic 108
Diana, Princess 72–3
domains
  contextual resources 48, 50
  individual behaviour 48–9
  psychobiography 43–4
  relations of power 49–50
  situated activity 44–7
  social settings 14, 47
  theory and research 115–16
domination
  control strategies 53
  crime 99–101
  over-control 112
  part of spectrum of control 60, 61, 64
dramas, control 57
dualism of agency and structure 8–9

emotion
  and agency 12–13
  benign control 71–3
  crime 101
  current life situation 93–4
  interactional exchanges 52
  mutual pacts 54–5
  and power 5–6
  reading others' 30–1, 100
  self-identity 24–5
  work 63, 74, 75–6
emotional abuse 76–7
emotional blackmail 29, 57, 79–81, 111
emotional intelligence 30–1, 55–6
emotional labour 74, 75
emotional terrorism 78–9, 81, 83,
    99, 101, 111–12
empathy 99–100
encounters, social 38–58
enrolment 55–6
environment, personal control 28–9
executive self 26–7
exploitative control
  agency 13
  contrast with benign control 105
  emotional abuse 76–7

exploitative control *cont.*
  introduction 1, 2
  part of spectrum of control
      60–2, 63–4, 87–8
  psycho-social development 28–9
  seduction 53

failures of control 89–103, 112–13
family relationships 72–3, 81–2
flight attendants 55, 74
Foucault, Michel 3–4, 5, 17
future unknowability 39–40

general theory 118–19
generic powers 11
Giddens, Anthony 19–20, 21
gift exchanges 109
Goffman, Erving 18–21, 46
grounded theory 117–18

happiness 89–90
helplessness 30
humiliation 86

identity 12, 24–5, 96
illness 94–5, 112–13
imperative control 108–9
impersonal control 75–6
independence 109
in-depth research 116–17
individual, and society 8
informal relationships 32, 63
innovation 15–16
insecurity
  addictive love 77–8
  anxiety 40–3
  emotional terrorism 78–9
  ontological 40–3, 97–8, 107
  self 25–6
institutional order 19–20
intelligence, emotional 30–1
interaction order 18–22, 46
interference 111
intimacy 41, 66–71, 73, 101
intimidation 57–8
invisible control 70–1
involvement obligations 46–7

killers, serial 85–7, 98–100, 102–3
kissing 45–6
knowledge 48

language 15
leadership 52–3
life sectors 93

life situation *see* current life situation
listening skills 56
loneliness 68–9
loss of control 89–103, 112–13
love
  addictive 77–8
  benign control 67–9
loyalty 75–6, 82

magnetism, personal 52
malign control *see* exploitative control
management, people 55–6, 74
managers, emotional responses 75–6
manipulation
  childhood development 28–9
  control strategies 56–7
  emotional abuse 76–7
  emotional blackmail 79–81
  pathological control 61, 63–4
marriage 79
mastery, personal 29
meaning 96, 97
men, sexual pleasure 71
mental illness
  blame 101–2
  depression 91, 95–7
  loss of control 112–13
  psychotic 97, 98
meta-messages 56
mixed-motive human behaviour 62
moods *see* emotion
murder, serial 85–7, 98–100, 102–3
mutual benign control 60, 61, 62
  balance of power 90
  essential feature of human
    behaviour 104–9
  romantic relationships 67–9
mutual pacts 54–5

negative significance 33–4
networks of relationships 93–4, 96
Nilsen, Dennis 86–7, 98–9
non-verbal communication 30–1, 56
notoriety 33–4

ontological insecurity 40–3, 97–8, 107
open-ended control 108
over-control 61, 63–4, 111–12

pacts, mutual 54–5
paranoia 98, 113
parental control 81–2
pathological control 61, 63–4, 72–3, 76
  see also individual types
people management 55–6

personal appeals 31–2
personal control 24–37, 38–40,
  94–5, 112–13
personal magnetism 52
personal mastery 29
personal significance 32–3
planning 39–40
positional control 31, 61, 62–3, 74–5
possessiveness 68
power
  discursive practice 4
  emotion 5–6
  inequalities 108–9
  interpersonal 49–51
  romantic relationships 67–9
  social sources 17
  spectrum of control 59–64
  structural phenomenon 3, 4
powerlessness 91, 94, 95–7
powers *see* variable capacities
practices *see* social practices
precedent, social interaction 16
presence/availability 45
prioritization 26–7
projected encounters 39–40
psychobiography 10, 43–4, 92
psychological terrorism *see* emotional
  terrorism
psychology, personal control 24–37
psychotic mental disorders 97, 98, 113

Rawls, A. 20, 21–2
rehearsal of projected encounters
  39–40
rejection 91, 99
relatedness 30, 109
relationships
  addictive love 77–8
  dual nature 15–16
  emotional abuse 76–7
  equitable reciprocity 110
  intrinsic to participant activity 44
  networks 93–4, 96
  powerlessness 95–6
  romantic 67–9
  serial killers 86–7
repressive control 61, 64, 82
reproduced character of society
  16, 17–18
research and theory development
  115–21
revenge 91
romance 67–9
routines 107
rules 19, 46–7, 55

schizophrenia 97, 98, 113
scripts 39–40
secrets
   emotional blackmail 80, 111
   family relationships 81–2
   women abuse 83
sectors, life 93
security
   see also insecurity
   self 25–6
seduction 53–4
self
   executive centre 26–7
   interaction order 19
   ontological insecurity 40–3
   security 25–6
   society 35–6
self-blame 101–2
self-centredness 56–7
self-confidence 26, 41
self-control 13, 31
self-esteem 26, 41, 86
self-identity 12, 24–5, 96
separateness 30, 109
serial murder 85–7, 98–100, 102–3
sexual pleasure 69–71
significance 32–4
situated activity
   agency 11–12
   in context of other domains 2–3, 22
   creativity 18
   individuals and relationships 44–7
   link between individuals and
      society 22
   marked by arrival and departure of
      participants 44–5
   power 49–50
social agency 9–10
   see also agency
social connectedness 109
social constructionism 36
social domains *see* domains
social encounters 38–58
social interaction 104–9
social practices 8–9

social reality 3, 36
social settings 14, 47
society
   relationship of individual to 8
   and self 35–6
soft manipulative techniques 64
   see also manipulation
speculative theories 117
strategies of control 51–8, 61
stress 94–5, 112
structure 14–15
   see also agency–structure
subjective reality 36
submissiveness 68, 70–1, 83
suggestive control 108
suicide 113
sulking 79

terrorism, emotional 78–9, 81, 83,
      99, 101, 111–12
theory development 115–21
theory-testing research 117, 119
threats 25–6
transformative capacity 9–10, 11
trust 67

uncertainty 35, 38–40, 96–7, 106
unpredictability 35, 39–40

variable capacities 10, 11
violence 53, 57–8
   see also serial murder
visible control 70
vulnerability 80, 111

women
   abuse 83
   sexual pleasure 70–1
work
   emotions 74, 75
   impersonal control 75–6
   informal relationships 63
   loss of control 94–5
   positional control 74–5